Kanashibari:
True Encounters with the Paranormal In Japan

By
Thomas Bauerle

Cover photo by Edward Scruggs. Photo editing and cropping - NIck Edges and Tuesday Bauerle. Cover art model - Dani Koto.

ISBN - 978-0-9961972-5-0

To the people who have seen, and the people who know:
know that you are not alone.

Table of Contents

A Move, An escape, An Auspicious New Home

As a partial explanation for why I became so interested in seeking out and collecting true ghost stories, I felt it only appropriate that I relate one of the many encounters I have personally had with the supernatural. Ever since childhood, I have seen and felt things that most people would consider not a part of everyday experience. I originally neither sought out nor had any inclination to learn about such things, but repeated experiences of this type made me want to understand more about what I was seeing and feeling. As one of my friends said, *"Weird things just seem to happen to you."* So, I thought I would open this series of tales with one of the most recent and most intense situations to which both my family and I have been witness.

Recently our family moved from the upscale Kakuozan district of Nagoya to the homier atmosphere of Aratamabashi. There were several compelling reasons for the redeployment: the old house was stately but dark and gloomy inside; the new house was light and airy with big long rooms that gave a feeling of flowing into one another, with a huge balcony on the second floor and an entire roof sculpted into a wooden barbeque deck. The old house had rude, up-tight, and unkind neighbors on two sides; the new house had smiling laid-back residents eager to help answer any questions we might come up with about the new neighborhood. The old neighbors never talked to us, or to each other; the new neighbors walked big loveable dogs down the streets each evening as they greeted each other and laughed together. The new rent was cheaper, and it was a much shorter train ride to work.

But even more importantly, we moved to escape the escalating annoyance of whatever bothersome spirits inhabited the old place. They were really getting out of hand.

When I first moved into the old house eight years ago, I was single and happy to score such a roomy place for such cheap rent. The owners were a lovely Japanese couple I had known for a long time. They were getting old and wanted to move to a newer, more convenient apartment that they could more easily manage. Since they knew me, they offered their big two-story house for relatively cheap rent, no traditional "key money" payment, and no need of a damage deposit. They trusted that I would take pretty good care of the place.

And it was a great place to live at first. The owners had gone against the usual Japanese conventional understated style and had painted the outside a verdant green, which made it easy to spot on the street. Inside, I had two floors with eight rooms, four bedrooms, large bath and kitchen, and it even had a full-sized classroom attached where the owner's wife had taught traditional Japanese calligraphy to school children.

The house was a great place to hold dinner parties with friends, and the band I was playing with could practice there if we went mostly acoustic and didn't play too loud. It was a nice private place to bring girls. And most of all, it fulfilled my Midwest American need for space.

Then something that was sharing the space with me began to make its presence known. One expects an older house made of wood to mutter and groan as it warps and settles, but some noises began to be heard that didn't match the description of the usual old house sounds. One floorboard next to the bed would creak incessantly as if someone were standing on it and pushing it nonstop with a heavy foot. Several times I would be awakened from sleep by a loud thwap! On my pillow next to my head, as if someone were saying, "*Wake up and notice me!*" Soon my pillow was getting thumped so often, I would simply shout out, "*What do you want? I'm tired! Let me sleep!*" and then I would roll over and ignore it. One night I heard the beating of a large set of wings flying through the dark, overhead, and I felt the rush of as they passed just above my face. I turned on the light expecting to see a bird, maybe an owl, or a bat that had somehow gotten into the house, but there was nothing there.

Many times, I felt myself touched, my head, hair, or arm stroked with what definitely felt like a feminine touch. I had experienced ghostly happenings before, so I just accepted what was going on and went on about my business.

Then I met my lovely wife, Tuesday, in the Philippines, married her, and brought her to Japan to live with me in the big green house. And the weird happenings began to escalate almost immediately.

The first month she lived there, my wife would have frightening nightmares every night that she slept in the bedroom. When she fell asleep in the living room, they didn't happen. She began to be afraid of even going into the bedroom alone.

One lazy Sunday, my wife Tuesday and I both fell asleep in the bedroom, drowsing side by side on the bed. Suddenly, my eyes snapped open and I found myself wide-awake, as if awakened by an alarm, my body tense as if to ward off an attack. I looked up to see a woman standing above my wife Tuesday as she slept, crouching low over her, with a gentle smile on her face. She was Asian-looking, perhaps in her early thirties. She had long black hair, and was wearing a red dress with black designs on the blouse and skirt.

Tuesday began to shout out in her sleep as another nightmare hit her, and the woman bent lower as if to touch Tuesday or caress her. Something about the slow silent way she moved made me very uncomfortable.

"What do you want?" I shouted, and she looked up, smiled at me, and faded away from sight. Tuesday remained asleep, but her face was peaceful now, as the nightmare seemed to have gone away with the woman in the red dress.

The next day, I led Tuesday into the bedroom and attempted to talk to the ghost lady. *Listen,"* I said to the empty half of the room where I had seen her before, *"we are living here now. I don't know who you are or what you want, but we would like to live here peacefully and in comfort. We expect that you want the same. Please let us live here peacefully. Don't bother us, and we won't bother you."*

After that, the nightmares stopped for a time, and Tuesday was able to sleep undisturbed in the bedroom.

In the following two and a half years that we stayed in the green house, we experienced many more strange encounters, not only with the lady, but with what seemed to be other presences as well. It would take too long to write about all of them, but I will list most impressive ones here:

One day as I was lying on the sofa in the living room, I looked up to see a woman with long black hair walking away from me into the bedroom. Thinking it was Tuesday; I began talking to her as she disappeared into the room. Then, through another door leading to the kitchen came Tuesday asking, "*Who are you talking to?*

Coming home one evening after work in a taxi, I looked up as the cab pulled up in front of our house. I saw a woman entering the gate to our house and assumed it was Tuesday. I paid the cab driver and rushed forward to greet my wife, only to find the gate closed, the front door locked, and no one there.

For a while, the floorboard next to the bed continued to squeak and groan without stop all night long as if someone were standing on it and kicking it with a shoe. After a few months, it stopped.

We began to hear the sound of someone moving around upstairs when there was no one there. The sound of walking and furniture being moved.

The board in the ceiling above the dining table in the

living room then began to squeak incessantly as if someone were upstairs jumping on it.

For a period of about two months, we began to experience what we called "the midnight party" in our living room. During that time, on an almost nightly basis, at exactly 12:30 AM, two of the chairs facing each other at the dining table would begin to move and squeak as if two people were sitting in them, across the table from each other. Each time, the squeaking would last for exactly half an hour and then stop. As I have mentioned before, I have experienced ghostly happenings on many occasions, without feeling particularly threatened, but something about the midnight party frightened me very badly. At first, I would walk right up to the chairs as they moved, and stare at them, attempting to see anything that might explain what was happening, but I couldn't bring myself to touch them to make them stop. I felt a cold chill run through my body, my hair stood up on end and I had to leave the room. After recurring every night for about two months, the midnight party suddenly stopped happening, and the chairs never moved again.

My wife Tuesday was relaxing on the living room sofa when she suddenly found herself unable to move. She then felt a pair of hands running up and down her leg, steadily stroking it with soft fingers. She tried to move, to make the hands stop touching her, but in classic kanashibari style, she struggled to get free, but could not. Finally, she screamed at the top of her voice. The hands went away and she was free to move. I was sitting across the room at the time, and was startled by her screaming. I asked her what was wrong, and she told me what had happened. In what may or may not be a related incident, shortly afterwards, she developed a blood clot, or deep vein thrombosis in that leg. Thrombosis is an old person's disease, very rare in someone of the age of 28 as she was then. It required many trips to the hospital, intense medication, and made it difficult for her to walk or work for the next six months. She is sure the two incidents are connected. I am not so sure.

Tuesday had a particularly frightening dream in which she saw a woman standing across the street looking at her through the window. "*I'm not leaving*!" the woman shouted. "*I am here to stay!*" She moved closer until she was looking directly in the window at Tuesday. "*I'm here to stay*!" she shouted again.

We were eating dinner together, my wife Tuesday, our daughter and I, when suddenly the cap off an almost empty bottle of ketchup popped straight up in the air and flew across the room. Our daughter, being so young, laughed because she thought it was funny. For her sake, we laughed too, but I could see the uneasy look in Tuesday's eyes.

When I was alone in the house, resting in the living room, I heard a small object leap off the shelf in the bedroom, hit the wall, and fall to the floor. I actually heard it whiz through the air. I was not of a mind to go in and see what it was.

While I was napping on the living room sofa, I suddenly sprang up, wide-awake. There was the red dress lady, posing in front of me in a very provocative, sexually charged manner. There was something very, very malignant, and disturbing in the way she was showing herself. "*Who are you, and what do you want?*" I shouted. "*Go away and leave us alone!*" She laughed loudly and then was gone.

The feeling of being touched, pushed and stroked continued at various times. On my head my arm, my leg. My covers were pulled, my pillow thwacked. Then the touches began to be more like punches or slaps. Not enough to hurt, but a couple of times, my arm was punched hard enough for Tuesday to hear the smack clear across the room.

At various times, a white fog would appear near the ceiling of the living room or bedroom and then descend about half way down to the floor. It would eddy and swirl as if being moved by a breeze, but no wind could be felt. It gave an eerie, clammy atmosphere to the room. One evening, my wife was out enjoying a girl's night out with her friends. I was playing with our daughter, who had borrowed one of my hats to dress up as a pirate. She was waving a plastic sword around and we were having a good time laughing. She decided she wanted to be a fashionable pirate, so she put on one of my neckties and posed. I decided to take some photos with my iPhone and texted them to my wife to show what a good time we were having. My wife immediately texted back. "*Take a good look at those photos.*" She said. I looked again, and was surprised to see the white mist swirling around our daughter's head. It was rolling through and filling the upper half of the room. We had been too busy having fun to notice it. I quickly got our daughter involved in watching some cartoons so we both could ignore the fog until it went away.

In addition, the atmosphere in the green house became dark and oppressive. We found ourselves tired all the time, without energy. We, who had formerly been happy, optimistic people, began thinking in a negative, depressed, defeatist manner. Consequently, when we found out about the availability of the house in Aratamabashi, we couldn't move there fast enough. As we left the green house, we performed the traditional Japanese ritual of scattering salt across the doorway and the gateway to keep any spirits from following us. At the new home, we scattered salt in the four corners to keep bad influences out. Our new house is bright and airy, and full of the laughter, music, and noise that only we, the living make.

Introduction

Is there such a thing as ghosts? The question for me was answered a long time ago, because, well, I've seen them. No, seen is not the right word. It's better to say, "*I've experienced*" on many occasions, some things that can only be described as "ghostly" or "other-worldly" in nature. And so has my wife. And so have a great number of my friends and acquaintances. And so have millions of other people, since the beginning of human history. As one veteran researcher into the supernatural says, "*too many consistent reports span all cultures and walks of life to be ignored.*" (Wicks, 34) It is clear that SOMETHING is going on that defies conventional scientific explanation and has impacted the human race since, well, forever.

This is not a book about "belief" in the supernatural. This book is about the experiences of people who have had meetings with what they themselves could only describe as the supernatural. As I was collecting these stories, I never once asked any of them, "*Do you believe in ghosts?*" This is not a book about spiritual beliefs or philosophies. These stories have nothing whatsoever to do with belief. This is an historical accounting of what many people have seen and felt. This is a description of phenomenal events that actually occurred and the honest reactions of the people they occurred to, in their own words. Many of these people have no concern with or belief system that accepts the supernatural except for "*that one encounter*" that left them questioning the well ordered, easily explained world they thought they were living in. None of these people had anything to gain by telling such stories. In fact, with some of them, it took a lot of convincing to get them to talk about what they had felt and seen. They had nothing to gain, that is, except the basic human need to share important life experiences with other humans who will listen. Many of them finished their accounts with words like, "*I still don't know what that was!*"

This is not a book about folktales. When I told one friend what I was doing as I was conducting interviews and compiling these stories, he said, "*You're the new Lafcadio Hern!*" No, I am not. In his wonderful books, such as *Kwaidan*, Hern presented some of Japan's great folk takes about ghosts and the supernatural. Those were well known stories to the Japanese people, passed on from generation to generation like the cultural treasures that they were. No, this book is about brief, powerfully charged moments of personal experience. Something happened, and quite often, the reason or story behind the happening is not known. There is sometimes no well-crafted story with a beginning, middle, and end: just moments of surprise, shock, and wonder. There are no legendary heroes or famous landmarks. Only normal people caught up in paranormal circumstances. These stories happened to ordinary people like you and me, often in places in which they usually find themselves: in their homes, places of employment, on the street, in the local park. The kind of places you and I go to every day. And that is what makes them so compelling, and, ultimately, so, well, "scary". One cannot listen to these stories without realizing that, if it can happen to THEM, then it can certainly happen to YOU.

This book does not seek to explain WHAT ghosts are. It only points out that, if so many people experience them, some recounting similar stories, often with eye witness accounts from different parties unknown to each other, and at different times, then it is safe to say that ghost definitely ARE.

There are many different theories that try to explain or explain away spectral phenomena: from religious leaders, cultists, spiritualists and mediums, scientists, researchers and skeptics. Many of these arguments contain hidden agendas or preconceived conceptions, and very few are satisfactory. It is well known that many professional "mediums," "channelers" and "spiritualists" have propagated so many hoaxes and scams in their claims of their abilities to contact and communicate with dead relatives and "spirit guides," that it is hard to take anyone making such claims even remotely seriously today. These things are not what these stories are about. Within the pages of this book appear interviews with two *reibaishi*, the Japanese equivalent of "medium" or "channeler" to provide some insights into the Japanese cultural understanding of such phenomena, but very few of the people whose stories are told here actively sought out any kind of contact with the supernatural: it came to them, unbidden, often against their own will. Most of them would rather it never happened in the first place.

No one is a greater admirer of science than I am. One of the most important achievements of humankind has been the establishment of the scientific method, a system in which occurrences in our physical universe can be tested to provide understanding of how and why things happen. But many scientists refuse to accept that science has its limits, especially when it tries to look at the spiritual side of things. It is hard for many of them to conceive of spiritual phenomena happening at all, and understandably so. Their field is what can be reproduced in a laboratory, repeatedly observed, and measured on machines. And the spiritual is, well, un-measurable, defying description by either logic or mathematics. The spiritual, however, has been with humans much longer than science has, and it has done as much or more to define human consciousness and civilization as science.

So, when science considers the spiritual, it often gets things backwards. Scientists will measure the brain waves of Tibetan monks as they meditate, and then declare that it is the monks' ability to access a certain part of their brain that gives them the feeling of being in a meditative state and feeling at one with the cosmos. It never occurs to them that they might be confusing cause with effect, and that, when the monks break away from the physical world and reach satori, it manifests itself in the physical world by showing certain electrical wave patterns in their brains. Often the researchers cannot bring themselves to attribute the experience of satori, or the trance state, to anything other than carefully controlled brain chemistry. The very possibility of the explanation being a spiritual one is rejected from the very start. Yet people experience the spiritual every day.

To prove something scientifically, it must be shown in a series of experiments that it can be repeatedly observed, measured, and reproduced. It is pretty frustrating for the scientist that ghosts do not perform on demand, at the times and in the places where the researchers ask them. Yet people have encountered them in every culture since the beginning of time. This creates a problem for those who deny the existence of the paranormal. One of the responses is just to deny the people who see ghosts any validity at all. Troy Taylor, in his surprisingly practical and down-to-earth book on ghost research, The Ghost Hunter's Handbook, states, "*Scientists and debunkers, who insist that ghosts are not real, convince themselves that anyone who experiences one is either drunk, mentally ill, or lying.*" (Taylor, 11) But, as he also points out, it seems extremely unlikely that all the millions of people who have seen them (or all the people cited in this book) can all be so completely misguided.

There are those who have used scientific methods to come up with logical theories that might explain what is happening when someone sees a specter. Some of the more popular explanations include:

Sonic waves - It has been observed that certain ultrasonic vibrations (vibrations at a level we cannot consciously perceive) give people a feeling of uneasiness and a feeling of being watched.

Magnetic waves - It has been observed that some magnetic wave frequencies also fill people with a sense of dread and the feeling of a threatening presence in the room. One of the more extended versions of this theory points out that countries on the Pacific Rim (including Japan) seem to have more words to describe ghosts in their vocabulary than other cultures, so it has been proposed that perhaps the magnetic waves sent out by the frequent volcanic and seismic activity in the regions makes people see ghosts.

Hallucinations and dreams. - Since many ghostly encounters seem to happen at night when people are drowsy or half asleep, they are just seeing very vivid dreams.

Brain disorders - It has been proved that stimulating certain areas of the brain with a small electrical charge can create the illusion of hearing voices and encountering strange beings.

Mental illness - Disembodied voices, spectral beings? The person seeing and hearing them must be crazy. (Moore)

While these hypotheses might explain some of the reports of hauntings, there are numberless instances that defy any explanation other than the supernatural. And it is usually those who have never experienced a ghostly encounter who try to develop theories that explain why they can't ever happen. This is like someone who has never been in love trying to tell you that your passionate romance is unscientific and thus nonexistent. The great majority of those who come face to face with a ghost will insist that, indeed, the experience was real. (Taylor, 11)

Taylor points out that, contrary to the skeptics' beliefs, there is more than ample evidence that proves without a doubt the existence of ghostly manifestations, and that evidence is History. Not only have ghosts been reported with great consistency in all cultures at all times, from people in all walks of life, some of the more persistent hauntings serve to prove they are real occurrences and not just the mental aberrations of the people reporting them. He describes a series of reports where a family or a new tenant moves into a place and has a ghostly encounter. Curious as to what is going on, they then seek out someone who has lived in the same place before. From the former occupants, they get their story of encountering the same ghost with the same description, performing in the same manner. Sometimes even different generations who have lived in that place will report having seen the same things. When the same phenomenon is reported to have happened at different times, seen by different people who previously had no contact with each other, that is pretty compelling truth that what they experienced was real.

So, what then is a ghost?

Ed and Lorraine Warren, who have decades of experience in the field research of hauntings and ghostly happenings, point out in their book, Ghost Tracks, that it may be impossible to come up with any one theory that will explain supernatural happenings, because there seem to be several kinds of things that happen, all of which get lumped under the description of "ghost." Some of these come under the different classifications of:

Psychic or Spirit Impressions - When something dramatic takes place like a murder, a war, a tragedy, or a great joy, it somehow leaves an impression or recording at the place it occurred. The event is then replayed again over and over like a movie on a loop. This explains the very common experiences some people report of hearing the same footsteps, or seeing a ghost performing the same actions again and again. In this type of haunting, the ghost does not seem to be aware of the living people around it (in fact, there may not be any kind of conscious presence there at all), it just keeps repeating the dramatic moment for as long as the haunting lasts. This type would explain many of the most famous haunted spots in history where the former participants in the dramas that took place in castles and mansions, the sites of battlefields, or at the sites of brutal murders manifest themselves for years or even centuries, always appearing in the same way and performing the same actions.

Transition and Crisis Spirits - Transition Spirits inhabit the oft-told stories where a family member or a loved one has just died and their spirit appears to someone with who they have a strong connection, informs that person of their death and says goodbye. Crisis Spirits are when a loved one who has died appears to comfort someone in trouble or in crisis. These types manifest themselves only once and then are never seen again.

Earthbound Spirits or Specters - These are people who died in a state of great emotional duress. They are still hanging around because they are confused and not aware that they are dead, or they will simply not accept the fact that they are dead. They are perceived going about their daily business as they did when they were alive. This is the type that is most likely to interact with the person who also inhabits the haunted place.

Poltergeists (A German word that means "Noisy Spirit") - Poltergeists are entities famous for making loud noises and moving or throwing objects around. They have been known to pinch, bite or scratch the people who enter the place where they are active. For some reason, they often seem to have some connection with a young person in the house who is going through puberty at the time.

Other entities or spirits, good, mischievous, or evil - These are spirits that were never human, but forces that exist in the world we live in. Religious groups have called them devils, angels, jinn, demons, imps, and so on.
(Wickes, Warner and Warner, 35-44)

These, then, are a few of the theories, speculations, and hypotheses about what ghosts are. Which ones are true? I don't know, and for the purposes of this book, it doesn't matter. As mentioned above, this is not about theories or explanations. It is about experience. This book does not explain, analyze, or categorize. It simply tells the stories. And for the people who are sharing their stories of ghostly encounters, those encounters were so real that they left an impression on them that will last the rest of their lives. I hope they leave a lasting impression on you as well.

Japan and the Supernatural

Modern Japan is not what most would call a spiritual culture. Although it was originally founded on a tradition of indigenous Shinto and imported Buddhist beliefs, most modern Japanese will proudly tell you that they believe in no religion, no gods, and no heaven. Since the military government during World War II co-opted traditional Shintoism and turned it into a cult of emperor-worship to further their own political ends, religion has gotten a bad rap overall in the country of Japan. The occasional disturbing actions of crackpot doomsday cults such as Aum Shinrikyo, which released poison sarin gas on the crowded commuter trains of Tokyo in 1995 only add to the mistrust of any kind of organized religious dogma in the minds of the Japanese population as a whole. The average Japanese does not attend any kind of religious service except at funerals and on special holidays or festivals, and has absolutely no training or knowledge of the basic concepts of religious philosophy of any kind. Their concepts of right and wrong are guided by the very practical concepts of hard work and maintaining group harmony at all costs.

Most Buddhist and Shinto priests in Japan inherit their temples and their shrines as part of the family business. The Buddhist priests in Japan are especially looked upon with bemusement by their counterparts in other Asian countries, because they have wives and families and often eat fish, seafood and, sometimes, even meat. Their argument that fish don't really suffer like other animals when they are killed for food doesn't hold much credence with priests from China and other Buddhist countries.

Many of the Japanese priests become quite rich in the performance of their duties. Spirituality and the denial of the pleasures of this world, which are so much a part of the Buddhist way of life in other cultures, do not always seem readily apparent in the lifestyles of the modern Japanese holy men. And yet they are part of a tradition of belief systems that are thousands of years old and which Japanese people regularly turn to for the bestowal of blessings of good luck, good health, success in business, protection from evil, and very often the exorcism of ghosts and evil demons.

In a land where most modern Japanese declare that they believe in nothing, how can this be? It is something that the Japanese themselves don't think too deeply about. A typical Japanese will fail to see any irony or contradiction in stating emphatically that he doesn't believe in life after death and then telling you the story of how his grandfather's ghost came and said goodbye to the family the night he died. He can deny the existence of anything spiritual or, that we have an immortal soul but, at the same time, still pray daily to his dead ancestors before the *butsudan* or family Buddhist altar that he maintains in a prominent place in his home. During the summer *Obon* festival, he will set out food and offer up prayers to welcome the returning spirits of his family members who have died. If you point out that this action clearly shows that he does, indeed, believe in immortal souls and life after death, he will most likely look annoyed, ignore you, and go about his business.

It is traditional for a Japanese family to go to the local Buddhist temple on New Years Eve or New Years Day to perform *hatsumode* prayers for good luck and good health for the coming year. At the same time they load up on magical amulets and charms that they place in their wallets and in their pockets to become rich and powerful. They will buy *omikuji* scripts that predict their future. They will put blessed tree branches and other objects on their doorways in the entrances to their homes to keep out evil spirits. When one buys a new car in Japan, it is often taken to a temple or shrine that specializes in car blessings where a priest prays over it and gives you a holy amulet to hang inside the car to keep you safe from accidents. Every new building is blessed by a priest before it is opened for business or used as a family domicile.

Before taking the all important college entrance exam, many students go to a special temple to pray for success when taking the test. If you ask them, *"Does that help?"* they will invariably answer, *"Yes!"* If you ask them, if they don't believe in any god, who, exactly, are they praying to, and how can praying possibly help? They will simply look confused. If they discuss the topic with you at all, you will soon learn that it never dawned on them that praying for help and belief in any kind of spiritual being who listens to your prayer had anything whatsoever to do with each other.

Ghost stories and the supernatural are celebrated quite often in Japanese popular culture. The Japanese even have a favorite time for telling ghost stories: during hot summer nights, because the scary tales give you the cold shivers that simultaneously freak you out and help you to overcome the hot clammy weather that is so oppressive at that time of the year.

There is a long, long history of Japanese traditional

ghost stories that have been written in such famous collections of folk tales such as *Kwaidan* (which was also made into a famous movie). Japanese *manga* and movies are full of such stories, one of the most famous being the 1998 Japanese film *The* Ring, about a haunted video tape, directed by Hideo Nakata, which was adapted from a novel by Kôji Suzuki, which was itself based on a Japanese folk tale called *Banchō Sarayashiki*.

Even children's stories are full of tales that many other cultures might find too disturbing or strong for their own children to see. Many of the scariest thriller stories and movies are about hauntings in school buildings, involving ghostly events that threaten Jr., High and High School students. There is a whole industry (TV cartoon animation, manga comic books, movies, computer games) about the adventures of *Gegege no Kitaro*. Kitaro is a *yokai*, or spirit monster that was born in a graveyard and is the last of a clan called the "Ghost Tribe". He is missing his left eye, but his long hair usually covers the empty socket, and he has, of course supernatural powers. All of his friends are *yokai* ghost monsters, too ("*Ge-ge-ge*" is the jabbering sound a ghost makes as it wanders about). Kitaro's father died, his body decomposed, and he was reborn as a talking eyeball with arms and legs that rides on Kitaro's shoulders and gives him advice on how to fight evil ghosts. In fact, the major purpose for Kitaro and all his ghostly friends is to protect normal humans by fighting against the evil spirits that attack and haunt them.

If you think this sounds like the creepiest idea for a children's cartoon you've ever heard of, then, I would have to agree with you. But these characters are so beloved by Japanese children that they flock in great numbers to buy *Gegege no Kitaro* toys, figurines, books, movies, games, stickers and to attend huge *Kitaro* events and festivals. My son, who is half Japanese, when he was between the ages of about four to the age of nine, was completely entranced by these stories that would totally terrify most of the kids back in my home country of America. And, to tell the truth, once I started watching the cartoons, I became an enthusiastic fan as well. Two of the biggest reasons for me were, the incredibly imaginative parade of monsters that showed up as antagonists each week, and the original Buddhist-influenced ways in which the stories were told.

In one story, *Kitaro* and his ghost friends descend into Buddhist hell to rescue the souls of children who had died young. There is a traditional Buddhist belief that the souls of these children in hell are commanded by demons to pile heavy rocks on one another. They are told that, if they can complete the pile, they will then earn the right to go to heaven. Indeed it is still a custom in Japan for family members who attend the graves of children who have died to leave little piles of pebbles by the grave to help the children with their hopeless task. *Kitaro* and his friends descend into hell, overcome the demons in a battle, and lead the souls of the children up to heaven.

In another cartoon, *Kitaro* and his friends fight a terrible strong ghost who overcomes *Kitaro*, smashes him flat, and then cuts him up like steak and eats him in little pieces. *Kitaro's* friends are helpless, held in a kind of jail cell and are forced to watch their leader being devoured. The friends then trick the demon by telling him sad stories and getting him to stand in the hot sun. When he cries and sweats. *Kitaro* escapes from his body in the tears and sweat, reforms and defeats the bad guy ghost.

Very few American parents would see these ghastly frightening stories as being appropriate for the viewing of their children. When I asked my son, who was six years old at the time, if he wasn't frightened by these stories, he replied, "*No. They are yokai, not real ghosts.*" When I asked him if he would ever be afraid if he saw a real ghost, he got upset and had trouble sleeping that night.

It's a cultural thing. Japanese ideas and reactions to anything spiritual of ghostly are, like any place else, a result of their culture and history.

Japan's is a group culture that works very well most of the time. One look at its success economically, at the influence it has on the world at large, at the relative safety and well being of its people in general is all it takes to confirm this. But it is not a culture where thinking too deeply is encouraged if it is going to bring up troubling questions about the way things are done. You do things because that is how they have always been done and that is what everyone else does. Organized religion asks a lot of difficult questions that are not very helpful in general to the group ethic. As a result, instead of any kind of organized religious thinking, what the Japanese are left with is a system of ancient folk beliefs that are as much an intrinsic part of modern Japanese culture as they were a thousand years ago. They are followed and believed in because, well, that's how it has always been.

None of these beliefs is still as strongly adhered to as the belief in ghosts. When I first began conducting interviews and writing articles about traditional Japanese culture for such magazines as *Nagoya Avenues* and *Asian Eyes*, I often came in contact with a bizarre cast of palm readers, fortune tellers, faith healers, *reibaishi* (spiritual mediums or channelers), and ghost-busting priests specializing in exorcisms. The Japanese refer to people who have the ability to see ghosts as *reikan ga tsuyoi* or "greatly sensitive to ghosts". I was amazed at how many Japanese claimed to have this ability. And time and time again I was taken to haunted places where it was generally acknowledged that disembodied spirits made appearances on a regular basis.

Later, when I began collecting folk tales from my university students as part of a class project, I was overwhelmed with the number of accounts they had to report of their own and their families' personal encounters with supernatural visitations of many kinds. I began collecting these tales until I had compiled a portfolio of thousands of what were claimed to be "true" ghost stories. I would like to share the best of them with you here. As you read and enjoy these stories, keep in mind that the Japanese people telling these stories are telling them in their second language of English, or the stories have been translated from the Japanese language to English. I have cleaned up the grammar and syntax where necessary to make the meaning clear, but an attempt has been made to keep the feel of the original language and expressions used when telling the stories.

Japanese ghost stories have a style all their own that is very culture specific and they fall in general into several categories or motifs. One of the most common is the appearance of the spirit of a family member who has just died to a favorite relative who is far away at the time. This is presumably so that the recently deceased can give information about his or her death and then say goodbye. This information can be transmitted in any number of ways, by opening doors, telephone calls, or the appearance of the ghost itself either in person or in dreams. I was truly amazed at how many of my students claimed to have been witness to such phenomena.

One particular ghost that is peculiar to Japan is the *kanashibari* or "holding down ghost". This is a ghost that immobilizes its victims, often when they are lying in bed, and holds them helpless, unable to move for long periods of time. Sometimes it is accompanied by the appearance of ghostly apparitions, or voices, sometimes not. It especially seems to single out Japanese women as its victims. In a casual poll I took of my university students and Japanese friends, I found that about 1/3 of the women and only about 5% of the men had experienced such a thing. And many of the women had had this experience a number of times. This is heard of in other countries, but with nowhere near the frequency it is found in Japan. Why is it so prevalent in Japan, and why does it mostly happen to women?

Other favorite stories are those of angry ghosts who haunt certain spots where they met their unfortunate ends. The most popular sites for these stories seem to be tunnels in rural areas that are dark and depressing to drive through at night. In particular, the Isegami Tunnel and the Chosen Tunnel where many Korean prisoners of war died during its construction are favorite places for Japanese teenagers to test their courage by facing down the specters that appear there at midnight.

This collection of stories took on a more personal meaning for me when I moved in to an old traditional Japanese style house that was haunted itself. This story will be related in full in a later part of this book, but the circumstances surrounding this "true" tale of my own was very Japanese in flavor, and unlike anything I had ever heard about in any other stories related to me. My friends and myself saw the spirit of the young lady who appeared there on a great number of occasions. In fact, it became so common that I soon came to accept her as part of the family. One curious result was that, when I reported the presence of the ghost lady to my land lord, I found out that it is an unwritten, but accepted "law" in the Japanese real estate community that, if someone has previously committed suicide in the house or apartment you now live in, or if it can be proved that it is, indeed haunted, you can ask for and receive cheaper rent. And there is my final triumph of sorts. There it is, accepted once and for all by even the legal community in Japan. The Japanese DO believe! And, finally, so do I.

One final note: I have organized each of the chapters in this book into three basic sections:

Description - In the first part, there is a description of the type of ghostly phenomena being discussed, and a short explanation of how it is viewed in Japanese culture.

Encounters - The second section will give a series of reports of "Encounters" with this type of phenomenon that I have collected from many interviews. I call this type of experience an "encounter" because, often, it is just one brief moment when the person relating the event experienced a supernatural happening. It is not really a fully formed tale or story, but one short, shocking moment that occurred that shocked the person reporting it. The main purpose of relating these Encounters is to impress the reader of how common these experiences really are, and to make the reader familiar with what, exactly, this type of supernatural event is.

Stories - These are more fully formed narratives told by people whose experiences were more involved or complicated than just one brief, "*Oh my god, what was that?*" moment. These sometimes involve some background knowledge of the occurrence, or multiple encounters with the ghostly manifestations going on in front of them. Sometimes these tales are described in better detail simply because the people relating them are good conversationalists and storytellers. These make by far the most satisfying stories to read and think about.

I hope this organizational style will be helpful in allowing you to understand and enjoy the experiences being related in this book.

Gaijin and Ghosts

I was first made aware of encounters with Japanese ghosts through talking with my fellow expats (or as Japanese refer to us, *gaijin*) living in or near the city of Nagoya where I was staying and working. It takes a certain kind of individual to leave your native country and seek work and adventure in a land where the culture, customs, and beliefs are new and exotic compared to what you are used to. The expats tend to band together in a mutual support system to give each other tips on how to deal with the local government bureaucracy, where to find available jobs, where the best shops, restaurants and pubs are, to share memories of home, and very often to share tales of their experiences in dealing with the comical and sometimes weird situations they find themselves in when dealing with the strange new place in which they live. At the same time that they are enjoying the discovery of new cultural experiences such as festivals, visits to temples, and religious rites that have been practiced since ancient times, some of them also come into contact with many even stranger events and beliefs than they would have ever believed to be possible.

In the 1990s, I was teaching at Nanzan University in Nagoya as well as contributing to an English language Magazine called *Nagoya Avenues* as a reporter, editor, and writer. My beat was to report on the local music scene and also to seek out and discover interesting aspects of Japanese traditions and cultural events. This led to stories on everything from the Tagata Shrine Penis Festival, a fertility rite held at a local Shinto shrine, interviews with Samoan Sumo wrestlers, to a feature about a local theater group that did Kabuki to rock music. You might say I made a second career out of searching out the unusual and the exceptional.

Amongst all the other oddities I became aware of, every now and then I would come across some fellow gaijin who would talk about religious rites they had seen being performed to give protection from or to exorcise evil spirits. Others would impart interesting stories they had heard about nearby places that were haunted, or legends about local specters or wraiths that had frightened the inhabitants for generations. This greatly interested me as I have always enjoyed hearing about, collecting and retelling folk tales and legends from many cultures. And Japan, being a country with a long history of civil wars, palace intrigues, samurai uprisings and assassinations, romantic triumphs and betrayals among royalty, geishas, priests and peasants, is a rich mother lode of such stories. It seems that every neighborhood, temple, and country town in Japan has its own private specter wandering about in search of revenge or expressing despair over some wrong perpetrated upon it in life. All of which provides the material for great ghost stories,

But every once in a while, one of my gaijin friends would have a story to tell about actually having a personal encounter with something spooky or otherworldly. I always found these tales to be the most interesting of all, as the teller of the tale would always not only insist on the validity of the experience, but would seem to be profoundly emotionally affected by it as well.

So, the first ghost stories I collected were from my fellow gaijin friends. When I later experienced my own encounter with the supernatural, it would lead to an even deeper interest in such occurrences which would begin the project that produced a series of interviews and meetings among my Japanese acquaintances and students, all of which resulted in the collection of thousands of personal stories, some of which I will share with you in this book.

These, then, are the very first stories of otherworldly encounters that I collected as told to me by my gaijin friends in Nagoya City, Japan.

Mark's Apartment

Mark Miller's introduction to Japan was rather unsettling. He was hired by a company to teach English in a town just outside of Nagoya. When he arrived, he was placed in a company apartment or *danshi* but he was told not to get too comfortable; in seven days when the apartment across the way was vacant, he would be moved there. When he inspected the second apartment, he found it to be almost identical to the one in which he was already staying. Not wanting to unpack twice, he asked his boss why he had to move, as he was perfectly happy where he was.

"It's necessary for you to move", was all that he was told. So he returned to his apartment and settled in as best he could. As he moved round the apartment, he was surprised to find little piles of salt scattered on the floor, and strips of *shimenawa* (pieces of folded white paper that mark off sacred places in the Japanese Shinto religion) stuck on the walls in the corners of his room.

Later that week, Mark was drinking with another teacher, a Japanese man who worked for the same company, and he asked him if he knew why he was soon to be moved again so suddenly from the apartment he was in now to another one that was just the same.

"*I was sworn to secrecy*", was the cryptic reply.

A few drinks later, however, his companion loosened up and told him that the apartment Mark was presently staying in was haunted. Mark's immediate reaction was, "*Come on, get serious!*" but the other teacher insisted that he was telling the truth.

"*The lady that used to live there committed suicide,*" he said. "*Since that time, the boss's daughter and several other people have become sick or gotten bad headaches just by walking into the room. The salt on the floor and the Shinto paper were put up for protection from the ghost*".

Mark thanked his co-worker for the information, but when he returned home alone that night, he wished he hadn't been so curious. He would probably have slept better the next few nights if he had not been so knowledgeable about the history of the apartment. Although now he is not sure how much was his imagination and how much really happened, his mind was so worked up that at different times, he was sure he heard noises as if someone where moving about the apartment when no one was there, and he often felt what he called "changes in the atmosphere of the room" that caused him to feel sudden chills or difficulty in breathing.

He had a hard time sleeping every night until he was moved to the new apartment.

During the move, his Japanese co-workers insisted upon carrying the furniture on a roundabout route that crossed a canal because *"ghosts can't cross running water, and that way she can't follow you to your new home."*

"It was then that I realized," Mark says, *"that I had come to an eerie civilization with shrines everywhere and festivals for the dead."*

I found the story that I collected from Mark Miller to be interesting, especially in what it revealed about Japanese cultural attitudes toward death and the supernatural, but even Mark himself confessed that he was not so sure whether anything unusual had actually happened in his apartment, or if it had just been his over-excited mind playing tricks on him. It was a fun story to repeat over a beer with friends, but it was not a very convincing example of an actual run-in with the spiritual. The next few stories I heard, however, related incidents in which the people who experienced them had a much more direct involvement with something they were sure was real, unsettling, and not easy to explain as a part of any conventional sense of what is supposed to happen in the normal course of daily life.

Noel and the Exorcist

Noel Miller (no relation to Mark Miller in the former story) is a New Zealander who lived in Tokoname until recently. A few years ago, on an evening during the Obon Festival, Noel and a friend were relaxing outside his apartment. (The Obon Festival is a Japanese summer festival during which it is believed each family's dead ancestors return to visit them. During this festival, families put out food and drink to greet their dead ancestors and make them feel welcome). As they were talking, a tall man walked past them and, without a word, climbed up the stairs that led to Noel's apartment, which was on the second floor.

Wondering why this stranger was waiting at his apartment door, Noel climbed the stairs to find that no one was there. Noel's apartment was the only one on the second floor. The man had not come back down the stairs, and there was no other way for him to have left. Noel reported he got a "strangely eerie feeling" at the time. Twice within the next week, Noel experienced *kanashibari* symptoms. He felt himself held down by unseen hands while he struggled, helpless to either move or speak.

Noel's Japanese friends introduced him to Shigen Wakayama, a Buddhist priest at the nearby Tentakuin Temple. Wakayama nodded his head knowingly as Noel related his tale.

"*So many people complain of ghost visitations during Obon that I am very busy during that time,*" he said. He performed a Buddhist ritual exorcism in Noel's apartment and Noel experienced no more supernatural weirdness after that.

During an interview, Wakayama described what is

involved in a Buddhist exorcism ritual. He first prays to and calls on *Kannon-sama* (the Buddhist deity of mercy) to come and heal the afflicted person's spirit.

"*I don't address the ghost directly, but pray instead for help for the living person,*" he explained.

He recites a *ju-mon* (an ancient charm that originated in India, usually written in Sanskrit), and recites the *Kannon-giyo* (the sutra which invokes the help of the god Kannon and basically says, "*Kannon I believe in your power, please come and help us.*") If necessary, he may also call forth *Oyakushi Nyorai*, the "Healing Buddha" or the "Physician of Souls" to make sure his client is well both physically and spiritually.

I took several photos of Wakayama with the *Kannon-giyo sutra* and two wooden statues of Kannon-*sama* that he had used during the ritual, but due to human error on my part, they didn't come out. When I phoned him to ask if I could retake the pictures, he declined, saying, "*Those photos were not meant to be taken.*"

True Ghost Stories from Gaijin

A woman related the next story to me from Jamaica who teaches at the same university that I teach at in Nagoya, Japan. Her attitude is a little more accepting of the supernatural than many others because, as she says, "*In Jamaica, people really believe in ghosts and the ability to command spirits.*" Even though the entity she encountered was in her office at the school where she works in Japan her reaction to it was shaped by the culture she grew up in in Jamaica. Here is her story in her own words:

Venecia's Story

In Jamaica, they really believe in ghosts. My mother has seen one and my aunt often sees things. We had a grand uncle who had died. My aunt had a dream in which he appeared to her and said, "I'm getting wet." She went to his grave and there was a hole in the grave where the water and rain were getting in. So she had it fixed. I remember when I was young my aunt would say things like, "There's a ghost out here, let's go inside".

Lots of people in Jamaica see "duppy" (a word in the Jamaican dialect for "ghost"). Many people also participate in the religion called Obeah, in which people really believe in ghosts and the power to command spirits. Also very religious people believe spirits can still be wandering around. There is that belief especially in rural areas.

But I've never seen one there. I'm not a superstitious person. I believe these things exist, but I believe a ghost has better things to do than sit in a room and bother me. However, three times I've had very strong dreams related to funerals and death, and shortly afterwards someone died.

When I was living in England, one night I dreamed I was on a plane flying from London and it landed in Jamaica. When we got off, they were lifting a casket off the plane. They opened the casket and they were saying, "Poor thing, she looks so bad!"

Shortly after that I called my aunt back in Jamaica. She told me about the ex-girlfriend of one of my uncles. She had been living in London. Her boyfriend had murdered her and the casket had just recently arrived there in Jamaica.

I've had these kinds of dreams three times. It just happens. I don't try to get deeper meanings from it. If I had a dream tonight about death, I would just assume someone is going to die because it has happened every time so far.

When I moved into my office at the university in Nagoya, I could sense there was something in my office. I had a "kanashibari". It had happened to me twice before in Jamaica, but I believed they were more medical than spiritual. When they happened then and I couldn't move, I thought, "just wait and it will be over". The first time it happened to me, though, I started reciting the Lord's Prayer in my head until it stopped.

The first time it happened to me in Japan was in my office. I was taking a nap on my sofa. I set the alarm for half an hour. When I opened my eyes, I couldn't move and there was a deafening buzz in my ear. I couldn't hear anything but the buzz. At first I thought it was cicadas outside, but it wasn't the season for them. It got louder and louder until it was deafening. And then I could move. And at first, I assumed I was just dreaming.

The second time, the same thing happened. I was taking a nap on my sofa in the office and I heard the buzzing, except this time, I saw a face. An older person made out of smoke. I don't know if it was a man or woman, but it was gray. I could see eyes, a nose, and mouth and the buzzing was there. And then I woke up. I could move and at first I thought maybe it was a dream.

But then I thought, I knew this wasn't normal. I don't know personally why these things happen to me; I just go on. But I knew a ghost and I cannot both occupy my office. It can come here when I am gone, but not when I am here.

I took a copy of the Lord's Prayer and put it above where I lay my head when I take a nap. I said out loud, "I don't want to be bothered by you".

I opened a window and said, "Get out!" I gave a little speech to the ghost about my office and said, "Either you have to abide by my rules or leave!"

Since then, nothing has happened.

I have to live and work here in this office. It can come here when I'm not here, or it can be wandering around somewhere at the end of the day. It's not something that concerns me, really. Although I can say, "There is something in my office"; it doesn't prevent me from coming here. . – Venecia Antonnett

Cornelius's Story

Cornelius Piros is a young man from Malaysia that I met in Nagoya through mutual friends. He had been a practicing medical doctor in Malaysia before he took a year sabbatical to come to Japan and learn the Japanese language. After meeting him at a series of parties and social events, he came to be a good friend with my wife and I, coming to our home in Nagoya many times for dinner parties, BBQs, and so on. Cornelius' encounter with Japanese ghosts occurred in Malaysia when he was a student.

I was a student at the Anglo Chinese School in Ipoh, Malaysia. It was a high school with a long history, built in 1893. At the time, I was living in the school dorm, in the student hostel called Horley Hall. There were many strange things going on at Horley Hall. While staying there, I twice met something that was not usual.

Three days after starting at the school, I was walking outside near the hall and saw a teacher there, an Indian woman dressed in a white sari. She was standing there with a sad look on her face. This was my first time to see this teacher.

So later, I asked one of the older students, "Who is the teacher who wears a white sari?"

He looked at me strangely and then asked me. "Does that teacher have short hair? There is only one teacher working here who wears a sari, and she always wears a red one. She doesn't wear a white sari."

After thinking a minute, he took me to the school library. On the wall were pictures of past teachers at the school. He showed me a picture of the wife of a former head master. Her name was Mrs. Threeth-ram.

He asked me, "Is this the woman that you saw?"

"Yes", I answered.

"She committed suicide by burning herself in a fire in front of the school. She killed herself because she thought her husband was having an affair with another woman. Since then, many others have seen her ghost walking around the school."

After that I was sick with a high fever for one week.

Also, sometimes the students would see Japanese soldiers who had died in World War II walking around the school.

One early morning, around 2:00 or 3:00 AM, all the students in my hostel, about 20 people in all, woke up because they heard a large group of people marching outside the hostel. There were often many school groups marching around during the day, but we wondered who was marching in the middle of the night.

We went outside and looked across the field, and we saw no one there. But we could hear the loud marching for 20 or 30 minutes. We heard men issuing commands in Japanese.

We were more than a little disturbed by this, so we called up the school warden. He said, "Don't worry, the last group of students who stayed in your hostel heard the same thing, and they were okay. So nothing will happen to you. Just go back to bed."

We later learned that the British army had occupied the

school during World War II. When the Japanese came, there was fighting, and many British and local people were killed there. The Japanese soldiers used the school as a base, and they tortured and killed many people there. The basement and the underground toilets were used as dungeons

I heard that there were bloodstained tiles in the underground rooms from the tortures that had happened when the Japanese were staying at the school. The school replaced the tiles many times, but every time the blood stains would reappear. Finally the underground area was sealed off. There were rumors that there was an escape tunnel down there that led to the river. Later in the war, when the British and American soldiers returned, many Japanese were killed in the fighting on the school grounds. And the students still see and hear the ghosts of the Japanese soldiers that were killed there.

The stories from the gaijin friends about personal experiences with the unusual piqued my interest in such matters. I began seeking out people who claimed to have had encounters with the odd and unusual and interviewing them. I also soon learned how to casually bring up the subject during conversation to see if anyone present had a spooky story they had hitherto been keeping to themselves. But it wasn't until I faced a haunting in my own house that I began to realize that all the weird events I had been chronicling were more than just entertaining stories. What still remains the most interesting part about my true ghost story is the way the ghost was introduced into my house. First it was seen by one of my students who then had what I can only call a prophetic dream about what was going on in my house, which she informed me about by a phone call. Later, my friend saw it, and then slowly it revealed itself to me, first through quiet whisperings and then by making its full presence known, as if to ease the shock of its arrival as much as possible. In most of its manifestations, it seemed to be aware of my presence and after six years of inhabiting the same house with the ghost lady, we developed what became a relationship of mutual respect and tolerance of one another. If all this sounds odd to the reader, I can only describe exactly what happened and let the reader draw his or her own conclusions. In all of the hundreds of stories I've collected, I've never come cross anything quite like the one I have to tell.

My Life With the Ghost Lady

When I began teaching at Nanzan University in Nagoya, I was lucky to find a house for rent in the upscale residential district of Kakuozan. The house lay half a block from Sugiyama High School, a private girls' school that every morning swallowed up hundreds of loud adolescent females in navy-colored school uniforms and then disgorged them all out onto the streets again in the late afternoon. Except for their enthusiastic greetings of "Ohayo gozaimasu!" when they met, and "By-bye! Bye-bye!" when they parted, and the high-pitched screams of "Fight-o! Fight-o!" during their various sports tournaments, the neighborhood was fairly quiet.

The house was old, a traditional style of house that most young Japanese tend to avoid nowadays, but which gaijin like me are attracted to because it evokes an old style of charm and tradition that has all but disappeared from modern Japan. The house was entirely made of wood and had a roof covered in ceramic tiles that were the sky blue color often found in ukioe paintings and the designs on women's kimonos. Inside the floors were covered with traditional straw tatami mats, and the rooms were divided by shoji doors made of opaque paper. I was especially happy with the back yard, which was about eight by eighteen meters (about 26 by 60 feet), an unusually large plot of free space for Japan, which made it big enough to hold small barbeque parties. A six foot cinderblock wall surrounded the yard giving a degree of privacy as I sat outside each morning to sip my breakfast coffee and enjoy the chirping of the local bird population as it woke up to greet the day.

Inside the house I discovered a couple of things that were out of the ordinary. For one, instead of a space for the traditional butsudan (a Buddhist altar for worshipping the family's dead ancestors), on a shelf in the hallway was a kamidana – a much more ancient form of Shinto shrine dedicated to the local Gods and household deities. There was a little wooden house where the household Gods that watched over the place were supposed to live, and three small receptacles where the homeowner was supposed to place salt, sake, and the leaves of a local plant regularly to keep them happy. In keeping with the customs of the place, I endeavored to do this, but I often forgot to feed the house Gods in a timely manner. I replaced the three required items as often as I could remember to do so and hoped that was enough to keep the magic working in my favor.

In addition, the first time I cleaned the house, I found that at every door and window, every possible entrance or exit to the house, someone had placed a golden-colored five-yen coin on either side of the opening. I knew that the pretty five-yen coin which has a hole in the middle was considered to be a good luck coin, that is good luck in the Asian sense of keeping away bad influences or evil spirits (as we Westerners might call them). So I left the coins in place.

The Kakuozan area was an old one. It was a very hilly area that had once been wooded and had been a picnicking spot for the upper class, the nobility, and even the emperor when he was in town. Now, however, almost every inch of it was crammed full of residential housing. And it had been undergoing renovation for some time now. Many rich people had moved in and erected large (for Japan) houses so that Kakuozan had recently gotten the nickname of "The Nagoya Beverly Hills". On our block, only my house and the house across the street remained of the quaint old-style wooden structures that used to grace the streets of old Japan.

I lived in that house for two years during which nothing unusual occurred, and had a very pleasant time, for one reason because of the kindness of my landlord, Mr. Katori. Mr. Katori lived just around the corner, across the street from Sugiyama Girls' High School. He had been a junior high school English teacher but was retired now. He was happy to have a native English speaker nearby to speak with and he was often very helpful in assisting me with translating official documents and tax forms I had to deal with as a foreigner living in Japan. The house I was staying in had been in his family since the day it had been built.

Then one day they tore down the quaint old wooden house across the street. I woke up one morning to hear a huge commotion going on across the street, looked out the window to see a gang of pint-sized bulldozers and power shovels tearing at the pretty wooden structure that sat there. Two days later the house was completely gone and a black asphalt parking lot was in its place.

The next Saturday night I had a barbeque party for one of my university classes. The students and I had a grand time frying various kinds of meat and vegetables over the glowing coals of my hibachis in the back yard. We sang songs, toasted kampai to each other with Kirin beer and played silly drinking games. As it got later, most of the students had gone home. Only a small handful of the most dedicated drinkers were seated on the tatami mat around the low table in my living room, exchanging life stories and talking about future plans.

Suddenly one of the girls, a student named Yukiko, jumped, spilling part of her beer out of her glass and onto the table.

"Yukiko, what's wrong?" we all asked.

Yukiko turned to me with a puzzled expression on her face. "Sensei Tom," she asked. "Do you have a big dog or something like that?"

"No", I answered. "Why do you ask me that?"

"Something big and white just went down your hallway," Yukiko said.

Everyone at the table immediately got up and stuck our

heads out into the hallway.

I even walked down the length of it, first to the right and then to the left, turning my head from side to side in search of anything unusual

"There's nothing here," I said.

Yukiko's fellow students raised their hands to their mouths and feigned drinking from imaginary bottles. "Yoparai!" they laughed. "She is drunk and seeing things!" They helped the tipsy Yukiko out the door as they moved to the entrance of the house, searched for their shoes among the pile they had left by the door, and said good night. While I cleaned up I laughed to myself as I remembered the earnest look on Yukiko's face while she was being helped to the door.

"But I saw something!" she protested. "There was something there!" They all bowed, said "Arigato. Thank you for the nice party", and left.

As I usually do after a drinking party, I slept in late the next day. I probably would have slept in even later, but at about 9:00 AM I was awakened by a phone call.

"Sensei Tom, good morning." It was Yukiko. Her voice had a nervous excited tone to it. "I must tell you something."

"Good morning Yukiko," I said. "What do you want to tell me?"

"Teacher Tom, I had a dream about you last night," she

said.

"Oh, that's nice. Was it a good dream?"

"It was a very realistical dream. But a strange one, " Yukiko said". A strange realistical dream."

I paused for a moment while I tried to figure out what this might mean. Yukiko was one of the better English speakers in the class but even so I could feel her struggling to express herself in her second language. "Oh, what was that?" I asked.

"Yes," she said. "I dreamed there is a ghost in your house."

I paused again for a moment of thought before I echoed, "A ghost? In my house?"

Yukiko's voice was gaining momentum now and the words began to rush out of the phone and into my ear in sharp quick gusts of emotion. "Yes. It is the ghost of a young woman. A young woman is there. She stays mostly in the kitchen. But she likes you. She is there. She protects you and watches over you. She is in your house and she watches you. She likes you. A very realistical dream. I saw it, so I had to tell you. You should know this."

I'm not sure how much time passed while I tried to process this information and formulate an answer. "That certainly was a strange dream", was all I could come up with.

Yukiko said goodbye and hung up. I mused for a while over the conversation that had just transpired before moving my thoughts on to other things and going on about my day.

The next Saturday night I went out drinking in Nagoya with a friend of mine from New Zealand. It was a usual boy's night out on the town. We hit several drinking establishments and put away a goodly amount of Guiness Stout, Irish whiskey, Asahi Super Dry, and Japanese sake. By the time we decided we had better call it a night before we did any permanent damage to ourselves, it was well past midnight and all the trains had stopped running. My friend was living in Tokoname, which was a ways outside of Nagoya, so I invited him to crash at my house, which was only a short taxi ride away. When we got there, he crawled off to sleep in the spare bedroom and I retired to my room.

When I staggered out of bed the next morning, I moved quietly knowing from past experience that my friend had a habit of sleeping late after doing a night on the town. So, I was very surprised to find him already awake and huddling under a blanket on the end of my couch in the living room.

I had seen him in the throes of a monumental hangover before, but this time I was surprised at the look on his face. It reflected, not only his headache pain, but also a look of mixed confusion and something else that was rather unsettling.

"Aha!" I said. "So you are paying for your sins once again! I told you not to take those last five shots of

Bushmills!"

He shook his head in a very deliberate manner. "No," he said. "It's not that. I couldn't sleep last night, because, I swear, there was a girl standing at the foot of my bed staring at me all night long."

I waited for some kind of punch line to follow, but when the look on his face was so earnest, I couldn't think of any other way to respond except, "What the hell are you talking about?"

"I swear to God," he said. "I could see this lady standing at the end of my bed out of the corner of my eye, but when I'd try to look at her directly, she'd be gone. As soon as I looked slightly away, there she was again!"

I really had no idea how to react to this. I ran all kinds of plausible scenarios through my head from, "You were just dreaming!" to "How the hell drunk WERE you?" to "It's time to cut back on the drinking because the DTs are starting to set in!"

Finally he took the initiative of replying away from me by saying, "I don't want to eat breakfast in this house. Let's go to Denny's."

"Okay," I said. And away we went.

I'm not sure now why I didn't think more about these two occurrences or see some kind of connection between them, but it was the end of the semester, and I was very busy finishing up classes, and grading final tests and essays. A few days later, I was lying on the sofa in my front room, grading student essays. I was feeling slightly drowsy when suddenly I heard a woman's voice whispering in my ear. The voice was softly speaking to me in Japanese, but I couldn't quite make out what it was saying. I could, however, feel her breath gently caressing my ear every time she spoke.

I sat up and turned my head in the direction of the voice, but there was nothing and no one there. The voice stopped as soon as I moved.

I shook my head to clear it, and remarked to myself what a strange dream THAT was! Fully awake now, I continued grading the essays.

A few days later, I was once again reclining on the same sofa, having just finished grading the last batch of essays. I dozed off. Lying on my back with my bed hanging slightly, face upward, off the end of the sofa.

For some reason, I abruptly woke up, my eyes snapping wide open. And standing, not more than two feet from me, was the most beautiful woman I had ever seen in my life.

She was a young Japanese woman, perhaps in her early-to-mid twenties, with long wavy black hair that hung past her shoulders and down her back. Her smile was kind and warm, and she was wearing a long white dress. For some reason, the thing that bothered me most at first about this apparition was that she was not wearing a Japanese kimono, but an older European-style dress with lace at the throat and sleeves.

Then I remarked how absolutely kind and loving the

look was coming from her smile and her dark eyes.

And then I went into a kind of state of shock where I could do nothing but simply stare back at the lady in white; my mouth and eyes wide open in amazement. It seemed like she was there for a long time. But I suppose it was about 10 full seconds before she slowly faded away from sight.

It was the only time I saw her full on, complete and whole, but after announcing herself to me with that brief appearance, she made herself known to my friends and me on many occasions over the next six years I was living in the house. There would be the sound of someone moving things around as if cooking in the empty kitchen; her subtle step and the swishing of the hem of her dress on the tatami could be heard as she passed by. On several occasions her shadow could be seen moving across the shoji paper walls. Lights would flicker on and off.

On one occasion, my Japanese girlfriend and I went out to dinner with two of her friends who were visiting from out of town. It got very late, so I suggested they stay at my house for the night. They bedded down in the guest bedroom and my girlfriend and I in the main bedroom. The next morning her two friends were angry with my girlfriend.

"What is wrong?" she asked.

"We couldn't sleep at all last night," they said. "It's your fault! What were you doing in our room last night?"

My girlfriend looked confused. "I wasn't in your room

last night," she said. "I was sleeping."

Her friends looked even angrier. "The lights were off, but we know it was you. There was a woman with long hair like yours walking around our room all night! What were you doing there?"

The friends looked doubtful when we told them it was the ghost lady who had kept them up, as if we were trying to play some strange joke on them. When they realized we were serious, they quickly decided to leave.

Finally I decided I had to find out who this woman was that had taken over my house. So I went to see the landlord, Mr. Katori. When they saw me at their door, he and his wife gladly invited me in as they had on so many other occasions.

"Katori-san," I asked, "has anyone ever committed suicide or died under strange circumstances in my house?"

Mr. Katori looked upset. "Why do you ask such a question?"

"There's a ghost in the house. A young lady. My friends and I have seen her many times."

An angry look came over Mr. Katori's face. He stomped out of the room and into his kitchen and began talking in a loud voice with his wife. This was confusing to me, as Mr. Katori had always been a most kind, and mild-mannered man. A few minutes later, he came back into the living room and shouted at me, "No cheap rent!"

It took a few more minutes of intense conversation before I was made to understand the cause of his anger. I learned that in Japan, if there was a suicide, a strange death or reports of a ghost in the house or apartment you are renting, you can legally ask for cheap rental payments because the place is considered damaged.

Mr. Katori thought I was making up a story in order to trick him and get cheaper rent.

His anger dissipated when I broke into uncontrollable laughter. "No, no, no!" I said. "The rent is fine. I actually kind of like having my own ghost. I just want to know who this woman is who is haunting my house."

After thinking to himself for a moment, Mr. Katori said, "No one died strangely in that house", but in the house across the street, when I was a young boy, about 1930 or so, there was a most beautiful girl living there. She was a teacher at the girls' high school up the street. She was lovely and kind, and everybody loved her. She used to wear those frilly European dresses. They were popular then. One day she committed suicide, and hanged herself by a rope from the rafters. No one ever knew why. Everybody was shocked because she had always seemed so happy, so perfect. I think her ghost was haunting that house across the street. And when they tore it down, she had no place to stay, so she came across the street to your house."

We'll never know if that's who she was, but it was a story that seemed to fit the experiences I had been having in my house. I lived in that quaint little house for six more years and became used to having the ghost lady around. I never really saw her full on again like the first time, but occasionally I would still hear her walking around, her long dress swishing over the straw tatami mats, and sometimes I would see her shadow again on the paper shoji doors dividing the rooms.

And, yes, I did get the feeling that she liked me and was watching over me.
I even had one girlfriend break up with me because of the ghost lady.
"I no stay at your house no more," the girlfriend said. "The ghost lady don't like me. She won't let me sleep." And what I found out about the girlfriend later confirmed that the ghost lady was, indeed, looking out for me.

Later I moved away to a bigger, newer house. Shortly after I moved out, they knocked down my old house and put up an apartment building. I didn't move very far away, and now when I walk to the convenience store, I have to walk by where the old house used to stand. Every time I pass, I pause in front of the place and almost expect to see her standing smiling in the doorway.

I hope she's at peace now and gone on to a more peaceful rest, or wherever it is she's supposed to go. To tell the truth, I kind of miss her, even now.

When I would relate my story to my friends, many of them told me of their own experiences with the supernatural. Some of them, especially the Japanese I interviewed, even seemed relieved to have someone they could talk to about what had happened to them. They were happy to have met someone who was willing to listen and take their stories seriously. I have found, that in the presence of accepting and non-judgmental people, in any gathering, about one third of those present have had something other-worldly happen to them that they can't explain. Not that many people can be crazy. So when you ask, *"Do ghosts exist?"* My answer would be, *"Without a doubt, and they are encountered by some people on an everyday basis."* What follow are the stories of those who have had such encounters. I hope that you, too, can be accepting and nonjudgmental about what they have to say.

Kanashibari

A *kanashibari* is a type of ghost often encountered in Japan, which seems to manifest itself mostly to Japanese women. The term *kanashibari* is derived from the Japanese words *kana,* which means "metal" or "hardware", and *shibari,* which comes from the verb meaning "to tie down". Literally it means "something that ties you down with unbreakable metal bonds", or, as some times put more poetically, "tied down with golden bonds". A *kanashibari* is a ghost that comes upon you while you are sleeping and holds you down so that you are unable to move, speak, or cry out until it decides to leave. An informal survey I conducted among students and friends showed that about a third of Japanese women and only about 5% of Japanese men have experienced a *kanashibari* at some time in their lives. In fact it is so common a phenomena in Japan that virtually every time the subject has come up in conversation there have been at least one or two women present that have experienced it, and very often some of them have suffered such attacks several times or more. Out of all the thousands of tales of experiences with the supernatural I have collected in Japan, by far the most common story was about meeting a *kanashibari.*

A *kanashibari* usually happens to its victim when she is sleeping. Suddenly she wakes up and finds that, although her mind seems to be fully awake, her body is unable to move. This condition can continue for anywhere from a few minutes to an hour and it can be an experience that creates an acute sense of panic and terror. In addition, many victims also claim to actually see ghosts and hear voices. Dead family members, who whisper in their ears, instructing them to perform some task that will enable their restless souls to find peace, visit some of them.

There have been several theories put forth to explain this phenomenon: one is that the person isn't mentally awake at all, but dreams the whole experience. Almost every person who has experienced one, however, insists that the experience was very real and that they were fully awake and cognizant of what was going on. Some theorists are ready to point out that, in a culture like Japan's where people normally work 16 hour days, seven days a week, it is only natural that some times people would find themselves so exhausted that it would be difficult for their weary bodies to move upon first awakening. This, however, doesn't explain the visions and sounds that occur with many of these experiences.

Modern science has made some attempts to explain such happenings. Oliver Sacks, a professor of neurology at the New York university School of Medicine, in his book, "Hallucinations", gives some psychology-based explanations for what he terms as "near sleep hallucinations". One condition known as a *hypnagogic dream* occurs just before a person falls asleep. It often features "quasi-hallucinations" that sometimes include noises and the appearance of faces. They are often seen like dreams in the dark with the eyes closed. However, he is quick to point out that, "they are not perceived as real, and they are not projected into external space". (Sacks, 208). Which does not account for the insistence by most *kanashibari* victims that what they saw and experienced was very real, and not a dream or hallucination.

Sacks also mention another form of "hallucination" which is termed a *hypnopompic hallucination*." A *hypnopompic hallucination* occurs just after a person has awakened. According to Sacks:

Hypnopompic hallucinations are often seen with open eyes, in bright illumination; they are frequently projected into external space and seem to be totally solid and real. (Sacks, 210).

A condition known as "sleep paralysis" is also talked about in which the newly awakened person is paralyzed and unable to move. They sometimes feel a pressure on their chests and find it difficult to breathe, which is the perfect description of a *kanashibari*. Sacks also tells us that there are often accompanying hallucinations of an old woman, or "night hag" who sometimes approaches them, climbs on their chest and "rides" them. Which is exactly what a number of *kanashibari* victims claim to have experienced. (Sacks, 228)

But when reading the reports of the psychologists who have researched such things, one is struck by a very important fact. They merely *describe* what the person sees and experiences, and they have no explanation for what it *is* or *why* it happens. Particularly disturbing is the lack of explanation for why most of the people experiencing "sleep paralysis" have such similar experiences. If they were really just random "hallucinations", why is everyone seeing the same things in such a consistent pattern? People's hallucinations, like people's dreams, are very individual. Why do so many *kanashibari* victims see an old woman, or a ghostly figure, approaching them, and holding them down? Why not see a purple panda, or a zombie tomato? It seems to be beyond most psychologists to look to any kind of spiritual explanation, as many of them do not acknowledge the existence of anything spiritual. Doesn't it make much more sense to consider that, instead of everyone's brains having the exact same hallucination or dream, there may be something real at work here; that something might actually exist that manifests itself as a ghostly presence? Say, maybe, a ghost?

F. W. H. Meyers, the English researcher who coined the term *hypnopompic* in 1901, did believe in the spiritual, but tried to put it in a "scientific context". After looking into many such cases of *hypnopompic* experience, he found his conclusions led him to believe in "the objective reality of a spiritual or supernatural realm, to which the mind might be given brief access in various psychological states, such as dreaming, hypnopompic states, trance states, and certain types of epilepsy." (Sacks, 216).

The sleep paralysis and strange encounters that are experienced by a victim of a *kanashibari* are well known in Japan. This chapter reports some first-hand encounters with *kanashibari*, the explanation of which is and probably will always remain a mystery. Whatever it is, it is very real to the people it happens to, and it happens very often in Japan. These, then, are the chronicles of meetings with the mystery that is a *kanashibari* in the words of those who experienced them first hand. Because they are telling their tales in English, which is their second language, the description of the feeling of being unable to move is often expressed in such dictionary-translation friendly terms as being "rooted to the spot," or "terror paralyzed." Nonetheless, the feeling of helplessness and terror it evokes needs no translation.

Encounters With Kanashibari

College student Miki Matsui relates a typical Kanashibari experience:

One night I was sleeping on my bed. Then an unusual thing happened on a usual night. Suddenly I felt something getting on top of me. I was so surprised that I tried to get out of my bed. Then I felt something pressing down on my head, so I couldn't get out. I couldn't open my eyes for fear. After I while I felt it crawl away and disappear. But I still don't know what it was.

Hiroyasu Shimura relates a similar event:
One night I was so tired when I went to bed. I fell asleep, but some time later I woke up, but I couldn't move my hands, legs; all my body couldn't move. Wow! I tried to call out, "Help me! Help me!" but I couldn't say anything. I was so panicked for a long time. Finally I fell back to sleep and when I woke up I was fine.

Many of the stories collected are similar in that the victim reports that he or she simply cannot move even though she will report that she is wide awake at the time.

My body, arms, and legs couldn't move! And I couldn't breathe! And I had no voice to speak! -- Yukiko Takahashi

I couldn't move my body, but I could look around me! -- Nagata Mizuho

Six years ago I was rooted to the spot at night in my bed. When I told my mother, she said she had been rooted to the spot at the same time! -- Yuko Tomita

When I was a child, I was often terror paralyzed. I slept every night with my brother, but he was never paralyzed. During those times, I was completely unable to move. It never happens to me now. -- Hitomi Ito

Many of the people who experience such things say they have no idea what they are. Some, however, try to find an explanation:

It happens to me because there is a graveyard near my home. -- Terahisa Shibata

One night my friend woke at midnight, but he couldn't move at all. Then he heard the laughter of a baby in his ear. In fact, his mother had touched a baby's grave that day. -- Mie Matsusaka

One day I went to the graveyard with my friends. We played tag and hide and seek there. After playing, we went back home. With night coming on, I went to bed. Suddenly I was rooted to the spot. I think the sleeping ghosts in the graveyard were angry that we had disturbed them. -- Masaki Ando

Being in close proximity to a graveyard seems to be a very common explanation for a *kanashibari*. In the cases where a person simply finds it hard to move for an indeterminate length of time, the more mundane explanation that the person was just tired or going through a *hypnopompic* dream might hold some validity, but in many cases the feeling of being "rooted to the spot" is accompanied by sights, sounds, and other manifestations that are impossible to explain in any conventional manner.

I have always been predisposed to be rooted to the spot at night. It has happened to me many times, but I don't have any extrasensory perception and I persuaded myself to think, "kanashibari is when only my brain is awake, so a 'kanashibari' isn't supernatural". But one day in high school, I experienced horror. That day, I finished practicing at my sports club and I went back home with my body exhausted. I took a bath and went to bed, but because I had gone to bed early, I woke up in the night. I am really a coward and afraid of the dark, so I wanted to get up and turn on the light. But my body couldn't move! I felt terrified and my body felt so much so heavy! Then I smelled the odor of a man standing next to me! I was terrified until he went away. In the morning my arm had a bruise on it in the shape of a hand! -- Hiromi Ito

Do you know the word "kanashibari" in Japanese? It is the condition where our consciousness is completely awake and our body is completely rooted to the spot. Some say that the cause is that the balance of the body and soul collapses. It is said that there is another cause that is interesting. When we experience a "kanashibari", a ghost is by our side. So when we experience a "kanashibari", we often experience psychic phenomena. Last Sunday I experienced a "kanashibari: for the first time. When it happened I could feel the ghost standing by my side so I couldn't open my eyes. It was a very very scary experience and I don't want to have a "kanashibari" ever again! -- Takahiro Ohara

Do you know the Japanese idea of "north pillow?" Japanese believe it is unlucky to sleep with your head pointing north because a dead person is laid out with his head pointing north during a funeral. Once when I was in high school, I slept with my head to the north as I was taking a nap. Suddenly I couldn't breathe and I was choked. I also couldn't move any more. The thought of death went through my head. I woke up forcibly and since then I never sleep with my head to the north. -- Misa Hongo

A *kanashibari* is often accompanied by strange sounds or voices. Very often *kanashibari* victims report hearing a sound like a "ringing in the ears":

My friend told me that he heard a woman screaming and his body became stiff. Then he shouted in fear but he couldn't hear his own voice. -- Kazuki Tsuboya

About five years ago, I met with a "kanashibari". I was sleeping and I woke up and couldn't move my body. My ears were ringing. -- Mayumi Hori

It was a very hot night. I found it difficult to get to sleep. A little time passed and I heard a ringing. My body got heavy. I could not move my body. I was scared, so I was going to make a loud cry, but I couldn't. I became more frightened. I closed my eyes. My body became unbearably heavy. I tried to move but couldn't. Someone called out my name. I cried for help in my heart. Finally I could move. I went downstairs and woke my parents. Now when I think about it, it is very frightening. -- Hisaya

My friend Satsuki is sensitive to the spirit world. One night, she woke up at midnight and found that she couldn't budge at all. All of a sudden, she heard the sound of children chuckling. The voices came from the ceiling of the room, but there was no one in the room. Then a voice said, "Hey, wait for me, Satsuki!" Then the voice stopped and she found she could move her limbs. -- Ikue Hasegawa

Sometimes the victim of a *kanashibari* attack has no doubt that she is in the presence of an *obake* (the Japanese word for ghost) or other form of supernatural presence because the attacker can be seen as well as felt and heard.

I never experienced a "kanashibari" until at 19 years old; I became a "candidate". I couldn't move my arms or legs or shout; I could only move my eyes. I felt very horrible! And my eyes found a more horrible thing. It was the shadow of a person that had no face! It overpowered me and held me down with a strong force. I closed my eyes and tried to shout and move. Some time later that shadow vanished and I could shout and move. Thereafter, I couldn't sleep for a long time. It was a horrible experience. And what is worse, since then, I occasionally have such a horrible experience! -- Daisuke Komori

My family's house has a Japanese-style room. My family doesn't use this room as much as the rest of the house, and the shutters are usually kept closed. So this room is always dark and smells dusty. It has white shoji doors and windows and it looks as if it gleams in the darkness. One day, something strange happened there.

When my mother was taking a nap in the room, she felt something moving there in the room. My mother couldn't move at all; it was a "kanashibari". Opening her eyes, she saw a vague pale figure walking on top of her body. It felt very light like a cat, but she felt it clearly and she couldn't move while it was standing on top of her. She has taken her naps in another room since then. Now, every time I see the half-opened door to the room, I shudder. I feel someone is there. The scariest part of the story is it happened in my own home. I feel this makes it much scarier than other stories. I never want to be alone in that room. -- Daigo Nakamura

I heard this story from my friend. One day she saw a traffic accident. It was a very bad accident; some people were injured and a woman was killed. My friend saw the dead body. The dead person had long black hair. Her blood was spread on the road. My friend saw her eyes. At night, my friend woke up and couldn't move. She saw the woman with long black hair sitting on her body. In the morning there was a long black hair on her futon. -- Shiho Suzuki

I saw a ghost at the age of 14. I slept at night in my room and was "tied up by golden metal bonds". My feet were numb and I couldn't move. A ghost was standing over me and looking at me. I could only see its face. The ghost's eyes were very big! Her face was very white. -- Yoshiko Mizuno

When I was a high school student I used to watch American NBA games at midnight. One night the game was boring, so I decided to sleep. About 3:00 am, I could hear someone talking out side my room. Then I heard *someone come into my room. I wanted to move to see who it was, but I was rooted to the spot. I became afraid and my mind went blank. Then I opened my eyes and I saw a young girl with a straight haircut sitting on my chest. I was very surprised! Then she climbed off me and disappeared and I could move.*- Shunsuke Kusumoto

(Editor's note: hair cut straight with straight bangs across the forehead was a traditional hairstyle for young girls in old Japan).

True Kanashibari Stories

Following are some of the more interesting *kanashibari* stories related to me told in detail. Every one of the people who related these stories to me seemed to be very concerned that I understand that they were very real experiences and not dreams. While telling their stories, they very often would make comments like, "I know what a dream feels like and this was not a dream".

Tomoki's Story

Every summer break at my university, I go back to my hometown. I always talk and play games with my family until midnight. One night I was sleeping in the same room with my father and mother. I seldom wake up at night, but I felt unusually cold and woke up.

"Did someone open the window?" I thought. But I felt colder and colder. "It's unusual. It's so strange," I thought. Then I was rooted to the spot by terror. I couldn't move. I was stopped by something. Then I felt as if someone's

awful eyes were staring at me.

"Don't open you eyes!" I thought.

I remembered that my grandma always said, "If you meet a ghost, don't open your eyes and don't speak".
I closed my eyes, but I heard a woman's voice that kept moaning and complaining. I could make out a few words, such as, "Hot, hot! Too hot! I'm burning up! So sad, so sad. . . "

Then I heard it say a strange thing: "I am taking your mother with me!" This so surprised me that I opened my eyes and saw a woman standing there, wearing a kimono. She was about thirty or thirty-five years old and her face was badly burned. She was standing there looking at me as I lay on the floor on my futon. I struggled to shout for help, but because I couldn't move, I could not ask anybody for help. Then my mother noticed my struggling and she grabbed my hand. The moaning woman disappeared. I couldn't sleep very well for a long time after I saw her. Later I told my mother about it and she said there was a local legend of a spiteful woman who burned the face of a young girl because she was jealous of her beauty, but my mother didn't know if it was true or not. -- Tomoki Fukumoto

(Editor's note: one good argument for the validity of Tomoki's experience is that he didn't know about the local story until he saw its victim first hand.).

Ayaka's Grandfather

This is my grandfather's story. My grandfather is, by

nature, very sensitive to spiritual things, so he often experiences sleep paralysis, or kanashibari. One evening, at midnight, he was attacked by sleep paralysis. He thought that it would end soon, as they usually did, but it did not, and it continued for a long time. After a while, he heard a human voice speaking, and he fearfully opened his eyes. There was a soldier standing in front of him! The soldier looked Japanese, and judging by his uniform and his wounds, he was someone who had died in World War II. The soldier stared at my grandfather's face and briefly murmured something. Grandfather couldn't hear clearly what he was saying. After a while, the soldier vanished, and grandfather was released from the kanashibari attack. This continued every night for the next week, and my grandfather couldn't stand it. He became tired and weak from lack of sleep and the effects of the ghostly visits. So he had a priest come to the house and exorcise his room. After that, the soldier never appeared again. - Ayaka

Family Troubles

The members of my family have been annoyed by sleep paralyses. My sister often gets a kanashibari. Once she saw a black shadow of a person in her room. It was at midnight. My mother has had this problem for a long time. Once when she was paralyzed, she saw a pair of hands reaching out to grab her neck. Another time, she saw a fireball flying around her room. After a while, it vanished. When I was a first year student in high school, I was paralyzed for the first time. At that time, I was tired from many changes going on around me, so I thought I was just fatigued and it was a nightmare. But it has happened many times. Once, I saw a little girl wearing *white clothes standing by my door. She reached out for me. There is a temple next door to our house. Many graves of people who died many years ago are there. I'm not sure, but there might be some connection between our troubles and the graves.* – Daichi Tsushima

Hitomi's Story

One night I slept in my bed, and suddenly I woke up. I felt as if someone was pushing me. I heard my bed creak with the pressure. I felt something pushing on my stomach very hard. Then I heard a song or some chanting. I had never heard that song before. The chanting was made by many voices. It sounded like "Okyo". I was very scared. I wanted to get out of bed, but I couldn't move. The chanting or singing went on and on. Then the song stopped and I could move. It was over. I took a deep breath. I woke up, but I couldn't sleep after that because I was afraid.

The next night I was rooted to the spot again. That time was different from the night before. I woke up because I couldn't move, but something was tickling me. Even after I came to my senses, something was still touching me all over and tickling me. After about ten minutes passed, it stopped and I became free. I thought my room might be haunted by spirits. Have you ever been held down by spirits? -- Hitomi Nishino

(Editor's note: *Okyo* is a Buddhist sutra chanted for the dead by a priest at a funeral)

Ayumi's Story

When I was a junior high school student, for two or three weeks, every night I was inhibited from moving. At that time, I was really really scared to go to bed. The first time this scary thing happened, I went to bed and I had nearly fallen asleep when I suddenly opened my eyes. I wanted to roll over, however I couldn't move. I tried harder to move, but I couldn't. Then, although, before I went to bed, I had closed all the windows, the curtains were moving furiously back and forth.

The next night, when I was sleeping, I woke up because I felt there was something lying on top of my body. Then to my horror, I opened my eyes and I was shocked! There was an old woman looking down at me! It was the scariest thing I have ever seen. I didn't know who that old woman was. She didn't do anything. She just looked down at me. I was sooooo scared! I wanted to hide from her, but I couldn't move, so I closed my eyes tight. A while later when I opened my eyes, she was gone and I could move. -- Ayumi Kawai

Yuka's Story

My mother told me about her experience. When my mother was a little girl, she was held down in the bed every night for a week. She tried to think of the reason why it was happening and she sensed that it must be her grand father doing it. He had recently died and she was now sleeping in his bed. So, the next night, when she was rooted to the spot, she said, "Grandfather, you died, you died . . ." After that the "kanashibari" went away and it never happened again. -- Yuka Ishizaki

Aoi's Story

I don't think I'm a very spiritual person like my friends who can see or feel ghosts. I never see them, but I am often tied down by something called "kanashibari" in Japanese when I am sleeping at midnight. This phenomenon has been explained scientifically, however some people say it is because of ghosts.

I will tell you a mysterious story, which I experienced when my grandfather died. When I was 14 years old, my dear grandfather passed away because of cancer. I was very sad and depressed, because I liked him very much. He really loved us kids. He was always kind and funny.

My family went to Kanazawa where he lived to attend his funeral and we stayed at my grandparents' house a couple of days. The day before the funeral, I saw my grandfather's body. He was lying down on a futon, like he was sleeping quietly without breathing. I clearly remember that his face was peaceful but very white. I burst into tears because I could never talk to him again.

After coming back to the house, I took a nap on the bed which grandfather used to use. My mother was watching TV in the next room. After about one hour had passed, suddenly my body was tied down by something. I couldn't move and even lost my voice, so I couldn't call out for my mom's help. I was being choked and was very scared. I could only move my neck and eyes.

I looked around the room as much as I could, but nothing was there. Then I timidly looked to my right and saw grandfather! He was standing by the bed, but he said nothing. I thought he smiled at me. Soon he faded away; suddenly I was free from the binding. I ran to my mom and told her what had happened. She said he wanted to see me before he was cremated. Although I was very scared at the time, I was glad to have seen him one last time.

In conclusion, I think that when people die or are in critical condition, something happens which cannot be proved scientifically. In this case, he or she might strongly want to tell something to you. -- Aoi Goto

(Editor's note: It's interesting that Aoi says she has never seen a ghost and then tells us a story about seeing her grandfather after he dies. To her there seems to be a difference between the two).

Natsuko's Sister's Story

I have never experienced anything like meeting a ghost, etc., and I also hate such scary stories. So this time I decided to talk about my sister's scary story, which she told me last week.

My older sister now has a job in Tokyo and last week she came back to Nagoya to have a rest. She is always working hard and recently she has been very stressed out and really exhausted.

"I couldn't get enough sleep even though I was very tired because of the job and also from the stress", she said.

One night she was in bed but she could not fall asleep.

She felt very bad so she opened her eyes slowly and looked next to her, and there was a woman! The woman looked so tired and was crying silently.

And then the woman started shaking her head slowly. The speed gradually got faster and faster. My sister was numbed and couldn't move but just kept watching the woman. She was very scared, but the woman didn't stop shaking her head and she kept coming closer and closer to my sister. And finally the woman went right into my sister's body!

My sister said to me, "I don't know what that was, but I think I saw myself. I think I saw my own spirit that night because she looked very tired." -- Natsuko Sekiya

Akina's Story

My friend was playing TV games in her room late at night. Then she sensed someone standing behind her. At that moment she was rooted to the spot; she couldn't move at all. She sensed someone approaching her from behind, but she still couldn't move. When her fear was at its peak, she moved suddenly and turned to look behind her. There was a woman in white creeping toward her. My friend turned away in shock and faced the TV. When she looked back, the woman was gone. – Akina Shibata

(Editor's note: I guess it was inevitable that, in a modern Japan known for its technology, video games would sooner or later be linked to hauntings as well as the more traditional settings for such encounters).

Yuko's Story

Several years ago, while sleeping, suddenly I was unable to move my body. I felt someone choke my neck and ride my body. Since then, these strange things often happen to me now. I always feel very frightened.

One day as I began to sleep, suddenly I was unable to move my body again. But at that time, I heard an old woman's voice. It was a loud groan. I was surprised and really frightened. I tried to move, but my body had changed to a stone.

Since then I always put salt beside my bed. Since then nobody holds me down or terror rides my body. The old woman hasn't come out again. I can have a good sleep. – Yuko Ito

(Editor's note: Scattering salt is an almost universal ritual to provide protection from unwanted supernatural forces. It is expressed in Japan in such traditions as the scattering of salt behind you after a funeral to prevent the soul of the newly dead from following you home. It can also be seen at the beginning of sumo matches when each wrestler throws a handful of salt onto the *dohyo* or wrestling platform to purify it and keep out bad influences).

Miku's story

One day when my mother was sleeping, she was rooted to the spot. It is called a kanashibari. She suddenly couldn't move at all. She tried to call for help. But she couldn't. Her mind was clear, so she could open her eyes.

When she opened her eyes, an old woman was sitting on my mother's body. She was so scared. Then my father, who was sleeping next to her, noticed her being overcome with terror so he shook her so she could move again. When she could move again, the old woman had disappeared. - Miku Watanabe

Takuji's Story

I would like to talk about a scary story that was my real experience. I had never believed in the existence of ghosts or spiritual phenomena until I experienced it.

I belonged to the badminton club in my junior high school days. One day, I was vey tired because of the hard practice so I went to bed soon after coming home. Some hours later, suddenly awoke and felt a strange sensation. I couldn't move my body! I couldn't even let out my own voice. What was worse, an object in black approached me. I thought that my time of death had come and lost consciousness. To this day, I don't know what that object was. I don't want to meet with an experience like that ever again. —Takuji Mitani.

Saki's Friend's Story

This is a story I was told by my friend. One night my friend was sleeping. Suddenly he was bound by something and he heard a baby's cry. After than something white floated slowly down from the ceiling. He got scared and closed his eyes, and the crying stopped. His house is next door to an obstetrics hospital. Maybe it was the ghost of a baby that died there- Saki Kajita.

Ikue's Friend's Story

My friend Satsuki is sensitive to the spirit world. She woke up once at midnight and she found she couldn't budge at all. All of a sudden, she heard the sound of children chuckling. The voices came from the ceiling of her room. There was no room above her room. One of the children's' voices said, "Hey, wait for me, Satsuki!" Then the voices suddenly stopped. After that, she could move her body. – Ikue Hasegawa

Chiho's Story

I'll tell you my true scary story. I went through a scary experience only once in my life. When I was an elementary school student, I was suddenly bound hand and foot one night. My heart beat fast. I sensed something was by my side. I thought I shouldn't look at it. Although I tried to turn my head with all my strength, I saw it. I was terrified. There was a very big face in the air. It was shaped like a quadrilateral, a dirty and bumpy face. It was just like a big rock. After a while, the face disappeared and I was released from being held. –Chiho Matsumura

Kana's Story

One certain night, when I slept, suddenly my body could not move and I woke up. I did not understand what was happening then. My body could not move at all, but I was awake. I tried to find a way to move my body somehow, but it would not move. Then I noticed something. Somebody was standing by my pillow. It was a woman who had long hair. She seemed to be watching me. And she said something to me; however, I did not understand what she said. I struggled fiercely to move and then I closed my eyes in desperation. I lay there helpless until I fell back to sleep. When I woke up, it was morning. The woman had disappeared. I still do not understand what I saw or who that woman was. Why did she appear before me? – Kana Nomura.

Daisuke's Story

One night I was sleeping. But suddenly, I woke up in the midnight. I wanted a to drink a cup of water, so I wanted to go to the kitchen, but I couldn't do it. My body wouldn't move. This is called a "kanashibari", and I have experienced it many times. But that day, something was wrong. When I opened my eyes, an old woman wearing white clothes was sitting on my body. She was grabbing my shoulders and looking down on me. I was so scared, but I couldn't do anything. The only thing I could do was close my eyes. Of course I couldn't sleep after that, I was waiting for the coming morning with my eyes closed. After a long time, the morning came. I opened my eyes and the old woman wasn't there. I can't understand who she was. – Daisuke Ando

Kanae's Story

Kanae's story is unique in that the feeling of a *kanashibari* attack is combined with an (almost) out-of-the-body experience (OBE). In fact she breaks out of the paralysis of the *kanashibari* experience to prevent her soul from leaving her body.

This story happened when I was still a junior high school student. It was a normal day and I went to bed as usual. After a few hours, I suddenly woke up noticing that my body was out of control. I tried to sit up in bed but I could not move my body. I tried to call out to ask for help, but I could not even speak. The only thing I could do was to roll my eyes around to see what was going on. At first I thought I must be dreaming, but after a while, I thought this must be what they call a "kanashibari" or sleep paralysis. There are many famous stories that say you will often hear someone's laughing or the ceiling will come down over you, but none of these things happened. I had no idea what to do to get away from this situation because this was my first time to go through this experience. Then I felt a weird feeling on my right arm. I slid a glance cautiously to my right arm. Surprisingly, I found a translucent arm protruding from my actual right arm. I was so shocked and frightened to find out my second arm and I thought I had to do something. Otherwise, my whole body would go out from me. Somehow I was able to move my actual right arm, so I grabbed the translucent right arm and shook it strongly. (This is the funny part of this story. Even though it was translucent, I was able to touch and grab it!). After continuing this for a while, I suddenly could move and woke up bathed in sweat.

I told this story to my family but nobody believed me. However, I can still remember the feeling of shaking my translucent arm and the fear of being paralyzed. This was my first and last time to have an out-of-the-body experience and I am really wishing I don't ever have this experience again ever. – Kanae Hasegawa

Hiroka's Aunt's Story

Have you ever seen a ghost? I have never seen a ghost, however, I believe ghosts exist. I heard this story from my aunt. She is little bit of a spiritual person. One day when she couldn't sleep well, she felt someone's presence in her room. She opened her eyes to see who was there, and she saw something that she had never seen before. It was a mass of white smoke. It was moving slowly outside her window. However, strangely, she didn't feel scared at all. She tried to get up but she couldn't move her body. The smoke didn't have a form and it made no sound and it had no face. In addition, the smoke didn't have hands or legs. It moved very slowly and it didn't seem to realize that she was watching it. After that, it vanished and she never saw it again. – Haruka Inoue

Chihiro's Friend's Story

This is my friend's story. One day he was at home alone. It was almost morning and it was getting light outside. He was lying on the bed, but he couldn't sleep. Suddenly he couldn't move any part of his body except his eyes. It was his first time to experience this thing (a kanashibari), so he thought it was interesting and was enjoying it at first. Several minutes later, he was still lying on the bed and was still frozen. He gradually began to feel fear because he lived alone. He was afraid that, if this continued, no one would find him lying frozen there until a couple of days had passed.

He tried to move with all his strength, but it still didn't work.

He remembered the standard saying "someone is beside

you when you experience a kanashibari". He looked around his room and found a woman sitting in profile at his feet. She had long straight black hair. Her head was bent so her black hair covered her face. She never moved. She was just sitting there.

He tried to ask her, "Who are you?" but he couldn't speak out. He tried much harder to move his body. He kept looking at her. Suddenly he could move! He had been trying so hard to move his body that he knocked his arm against the wall.

"Itai!" he screamed (ouch!). Then the woman disappeared.

Later he told his story to his friend who has the inspiration to see ghosts. His friend told him to move if he sees her again. My friend still lives there wondering if he will see her again. – Chihiro Yamagishi

A Friend's Story

This is a story I heard from my friend from junior high school. She was an elementary school student when it happened. She was sleeping alone in her bedroom as usual. Suddenly she woke up and she couldn't move. She was bound firmly by sleep paralysis. Then she saw a strange woman standing near the door. The woman walked slowly up to her. My friend was frightened so she tried to call her mother, but she had lost her voice. She wanted to escape, but she still couldn't move. When the woman had nearly touched her body, my friend suddenly got back her movement. She picked up an electric fan and swung it at the woman to keep her away, and then the woman vanished. – Name withheld by request

Arisa's Story

This is a story that happened when I was a junior high student. It was hot and humid and the night had a weird feeling. I was studying alone in the living room. Because I was so tired from preparing for an examination, I went to sleep over my homework.

Then I heard a loud, noisy woman's voice. I was surprised at the voice and woke up. But strangely there was nobody else in the living room. I wondered if someone had really been speaking, however, I thought it must have been only my fancy and I went to sleep again.

While I was sleeping, suddenly I felt as if something was lying on my body. I was really surprised and wanted to escape, but couldn't move at all as if my body had become stone. I wondered what was happening. Then, someone whispered near my ear. I couldn't understand what she said. I felt certainly there must be someone in the room besides me, but was too fearful to open my eyes.

After a few minutes, I had the feeling that whoever was pushing on my body had vanished. Opening my eyes, I saw there was nobody there. Instead, a big spider, bigger than any I had ever seen, was creeping on the ceiling, but it vanished, and the next moment the door to the room opened by itself. I was really scared at this, and suddenly felt ill, so I rushed to the toilet.

Though I never saw any ghosts, mysterious incidents sometimes happened after then, for example, I would hear a voice in spite of that there wasn't anyone in the room except me. So I felt scared and visited a Japanese priest and had myself purified. Since then I rarely hear any voices. – Arisa Hashimoto

Makoto's Story

This is a story of two years ago. I live alone in Kamiyashiro. In September 2010 at night I went to the tavern where I worked part time. I was drinking a lot of alcohol and I got very drunk, so my boss sent me home because I was not able to walk. When I got to my house, I was feeling very bad. I rested on the sofa and went into a deep sleep.

I woke up a few hours later because of sleep paralysis. It felt like someone was riding on my belly and I heard the small voice of a woman. I could not open my eyes for fear. When the sleep paralysis was over, I opened my eyes. When I looked out the window, I saw a woman standing on the balcony. The woman stood there wearing a black dress and she had long black hair. I closed my eyes again and when I opened them once again, the woman had gone.

This is a true story. I have told this story to many friends and they were scared. But I have never believed in ghosts and I think it was the influence of alcohol and sleep. Do you believe or not it's up to you. – Makoto Ohara

Keisuke's Story

I will tell you a horror story that I experienced. Early one morning, I suddenly woke up and looked round my room, however, I was not able to move I said in my mind,

"This is a kanashibari. Many people experience a kanashibari, so don't worry." When I said this in my mind, I heard a voice. It was the voice of someone laughing. I was very, very scared. – Keisuke Morita

Hiroki's Sister's Story

I'm going to tell you a story about my younger sister. My family and I moved to Kasugai three years ago. As soon as we moved, my sister began to be sometimes rooted to the spot by terror. She told me about one time when she couldn't move her body at all. She heard a strange voice coming from the wall while she was being held down and couldn't move. She has not been able to sleep without a light ever since that experience. She was not able to sleep in her room for three months after that. – – Hiroki Yamada

Yuma's Story

When I was a high school student, I was often paralyzed at night, so after a while, I wasn't afraid when it happened. One night, I was paralyzed as usual. I thought I should just wait until I was released, but then someone pulled my quilt off of me. I thought my sister was doing some mischief, and playing a trick on me. The next morning I asked my sister about it, and she said she hadn't been in my room and hadn't played any tricks on me. I was very surprised and became very scared. Maybe it was a ghost doing the mischief. –Yuma Suzuki

Megumi's Story

When I was sleeping in my house, suddenly terror rooted me to the spot. I couldn't move my arms or legs. I could only move my eyes. I wanted someone to come and help me, but I couldn't say anything. I had been robbed of my voice. A few minutes later, I was released from being held down. When I consider why this happens to me, the house that once stood in the place where my house is built now was burned down and then this became vacant land. After that, my house was built in the same place. I think that is why I am often sleep paralyzed when I am in my house. -- Megumi Takeuchi.

Michiyo's Story

The story of Michiyo Miura is one of the most amazing that I have collected in that she has experienced *kanashibari* on a regular basis throughout various stages of her life. Each time the encounter followed a similar pattern that manifested itself in three distinct stages that soon became so familiar to her that she could even sense when an attack was coming on. It is also interesting that she usually seemed more curious about what was happening to her than afraid, and she was able after a time to "challenge herself" to try different reactions in a sort of experiment to see if she could influence the events as they unfolded. At times she was even able to ward off the oncoming attacks when she sensed them coming on. Michiyo, who always paid great attention to detail, was a very entertaining storyteller. She told me about her *kanashibari* experiences during a lengthy interview during which she laughed and joked about them as if she were simply talking about any other normal occurrence from her past. She seems to remain more bemused than frightened by what has happened to her. She doesn't make any attempt to explain what she thinks they are, but rather merely relates them as they happened.

The "kanashibari" first began when I was 15, immediately after the death of my best friend's father who had passed away from a stroke. I had never met him, but I felt kind of close to him because he was from a small island close to Tokoname. His family ran a "menshuku" (a small inn) there. My family and I went and stayed there and had a good time with his family although he was away in Nagoya and wasn't there at the time.

When the first "kanashibari" happened I was in bed in my room at about two or three o'clock in the morning. I was studying for school exams the next day. I was lying in bed with the lights on. I wasn't planning on sleeping. My parents owned a coffee shop downstairs and I had drunk lots of coffee to stay awake, so my body was tired but my brain was still racing. But I fell asleep for a short time.

I woke up feeling as if my body was held down by plenty of ropes or as if I was sealed in a very tight plastic tube. I couldn't move any part of my body except my eyelids, but my brain was wide-awake and functioning. I heard a strange buzzing sound like fluorescent lights make and then the voice of a man calling from far away mixing with and coming out of that first sound. At first I wasn't frightened at all, just surprised that I was awake but couldn't move. The man's voice was very far away. I could feel the pain and struggle in the man's voice even though I couldn't understand what he was saying.

When I told my friends about it the next day, they were frightened by the story. They decided it must be the voice of my friend's father who had died a few days before. I thought maybe he was asking me to watch over his daughter because he was no longer there to take care of her. After that the same type of "kanashibari" happened to me in the same bedroom, for about five more times or so, always in the exact same way.

The "kanashibari" always come to me in the same way, in three distinct stages. In the first stage, I hear that buzzing like a fluorescent lamp. I still don't like fluorescent lights because of that. Then I can hear a man's voice from very far away. At first it is slow and strange like a record player playing at too slow a speed. I can' t understand it, it's like "Ruwawarrruuaarwar!" I don't really get frightened yet, but I can feel something strange is going on. Then the voice fades away. The first stage only lasts for about 30 seconds or so. It always starts out slowly. Maybe I can feel a little tingling in my body like when your foot goes to sleep. The voice fades out gradually and stops.

The second stage always starts suddenly. The voice returns louder, sounding upset and painful like he is demanding something from me. A big heavy invisible power like heavy air is crushing me. It's so heavy. Then the voice is right in my ear slowly shouting, screaming in my ear.

I still can't understand what he is saying. I begin to panic because I can do nothing but wait and pray, "Please go away".

The first few times I kept my eyes closed. I was frightened, but couldn't understand what was going on. I knew something frightening was going on, but wasn't sure at first if it was reality or a dream. The second stage is always longer--it's heavy, loud, and long. Then suddenly the voice stops, the weight is gone and it's over.

The third stage begins 10 or 15 seconds later. It begins slowly and gradually--there is a lighter pressure on my body than before. The same voice returns, but it sounds more relaxed. The voice sounds more peaceful. Still scary but more peaceful. I still can't understand the words, but it seems like he is saying "goodbye" or "that's the end of this chapter." It fades away.

After the third stage is gone, I am 100% awake. There are no hang-over-like feelings. I can move my body freely. I feel at a loss to understand what just happened, but I feel calm.

After that I had the same type of "kanashibari" under the same conditions about five more times: it always happened about 2:00 in the morning when I was studying with all the lights on when I was just trying to take some quick rest while lying on the bed.

After about the third time I was able to feel when it was coming. It felt like when you jump in deep water and you can feel the pressure on your ears. Or when you cup your hands over your ears. There is a change in the sound of the air.

Several times I thought about opening my eyes to see what was going on, but I didn't want to open my eyes and see the face of a ghost that would look at me and say, "Mita na?" (So you saw me, didn't you?) "So, now I have to kill you!" (Editor's note: this is a common motif in traditional Japanese ghost stories).

I had begun to think of it as a show put on by the ghost. There was the introduction (first stage), the show (second stage), and the finale or goodbye (third stage). I decided to open my eyes during the second stage, or main show. Looking back now, I think that it is a little strange that I never really became afraid to be alone in my room. I also didn't usually tell anybody about the attacks because, although I felt a kind of panic when they were occurring, they were happening so often, they were no longer any really big deal in my mind.

Finally the fourth or fifth time, I challenged myself and got the courage to open my eyes. I was curious after such a long time. The fifth time, was different. There was no voice, but the air was different like usual and I couldn't move. I opened my eyes during the second stage. I opened my eyes slowly: 1/3 of the way open. 1/2, 2/3 . . . so that the ghost wouldn't notice me looking and shout, "Mita, na?"

Then I looked and saw an old lady sitting in an old-style rattan chair wearing a white gown and with her hair all up in a knot on her head. She had on a long white night gown with fancy lace and ribbons -- all in white, but she was partially transparent. I couldn't make out the facial features. I could see through her like an X-ray. I saw her for several seconds at most before she was gone.

I was surprised to see a woman because it was always a

man's voice I had heard before. She left behind no special feelings or impressions. I just saw the figure. It happened quickly. I was not so frightened, just confused. I had expected to see a man with a very frightening face, but the lady looked very small sitting in that chair. Although she was dressed in western style clothing she was definitely Japanese or Asian.

After that, the "kanashibari" didn't appear again for about three or four years, when I was 22 or 23. Then I was staying in a different room, a bigger room, in my folks' house. I now had the whole upstairs since my older sister had moved out. Just like before these "kanashibari" always appeared when the ceiling light was on, or during daylight -- always in the full light.

This one was a scary one. The first stage was the same as before. During the second stage I was lying on the bed but couldn't move, but this time I felt something was there. I opened my eyes and saw a young lady standing about two meters away to the left of the bed. Her head was inclined and looking down. I couldn't tell if she was looking at me or not. Just like before, everything was transparent and I couldn't see her face.

She was wearing a white western style dress. She was looking down and standing with her shoulders hunched. She was slowly moving her body back and forth.

I closed my eyes immediately and then I felt the mattress sinking next to my legs, so I knew the ghost girl had sat down. I thought, "Oh my God! Now she's going to attack me!"

Then I could feel the girl kneeling on the bed with her hands on either side of my body. I felt her hands slowly inch up on either side of my body to where the girl had to have been staring straight into my face.

At that moment I screamed at the top of my lungs. Immediately everything was gone. But I am pretty sure that when I first opened my eyes, only for a moment, I saw the girl's face very close to mine. I still couldn't make out the features of the face.

After that, I was more afraid and I began to learn how to avoid the "kanashibari". At the first sound and the feeling of the air changing I would wake myself up. I would shake my body before it became completely tied down, and then I could get up and stop it. It worked a few times.

Then one night it didn't work. Six months to a year later, it was again about two or three o'clock. It was warm. I was lying down with the blanket off; it was only covering my knees. I was sleeping on my back. I felt the "kanashibari" starting, but this time I couldn't stop it.

I didn't want to see the same girl again, so I tried to move my body and wake up before the young girl started attacking me, but I couldn't move. Then I felt the blanket slowly unrolling up over my body; slowly moving up until it covered my entire body. Usually I couldn't move in this stage, but somehow I leaped up out of the bed. I ran down the stairs and entered my parents' bedroom. I didn't want to wake them, but I didn't want to be alone because I was totally freaked out. I decided to sleep on the floor between the two beds; my mother on one side and father on the *other.*

I thought maybe I could return to my own bedroom after awhile because probably the strange power would be gone in a few hours. This might seem strange, but at the time I was thinking that I didn't have to be afraid to be in my room most of the time because I felt the "kanashibari" maybe didn't really want to hurt me because I hadn't done anything wrong to anyone in this world. I myself had never done anything wrong for anyone to be mad at -- unless maybe one of my ancestors had done something wrong. I just felt that the power there was playing with me, or making fun of me; just teasing me.

Strangely enough, I woke about three hours later back in my own bed. I was surprised because I didn't remember walking back there. I thought I was still sleeping in my parents' bedroom. I felt very strange because I didn't know if any or all of it had been a dream. Did I make the last part up at the end of the "kanashibari?" Did I dream going down stairs? I didn't think it was a dream.

About six months later, I finally told my mother that a "kanashibari" sometimes happened to me and the last one was really scary because I had run downstairs to sleep in her room. My mother said that was funny because she had noticed me coming into her bedroom saying I had had a bad dream and wanted to sleep next to her. But when she woke up, I was gone and she thought she had just had a dream.

Sometimes I wonder if it was just my soul that left my body and traveled down the stairs. If so, isn't that kind of exciting? If your soul or consciousness can really leave your body and go anywhere you want? If so, this story is not so scary because I was able to travel to my mother and she felt it. So I feel a spiritual connection with my mother, and she was able to sense my soul. Isn't that great? My father was asleep and he didn't feel anything, but he's never exactly been the sensitive type.

A "kanashibari" has happened to me two times since then. Once it happened in Arlington, Virginia when I was living in America when I was taking a nap in the daytime. The three stages came, but no voice and I saw nothing when I opened my eyes. Just the sunlight shining through the curtains. The only scary thing was my thought, "Why is happening to me in America? Has the power followed me? Or am I encountering an American ghost?" It only happened to me one time in America.

Over the last twenty years, it has never happened to me again. -- Michiyo Miura

Seers

I am always amazed at the people who express their disbelief in ghosts with the logic of, "Well, *I'VE* never seen anything like that!" In the first place that's no proof that something doesn't exist. I've never seen the city of Paris, either, but I know enough people who claim they have for me to seriously consider the possibility it's a real place. Or at least that there is something over there in France that people react to that might be labeled "Paris," whatever it is. It's exactly *BECAUSE* I haven't been there myself and wasn't there when my friends encountered Paris that I feel I should acknowledge what they have to say about it, and I certainly would never presume to tell them my favorite theory about what *REALLY* was going on when they met Paris, because *I wasn't there when it happened!*

It's the same with people who have experienced encounters with ghosts. If you weren't there when the person had the experience, you don't get to dismiss it and tell them it wasn't real. In addition, if you weren't there when it happened, you have no right to tell the person that experienced an encounter with a ghost that you don't believe in his experience, and you certainly don't have the right to make uninformed statements on what you think was really happening at the time.

Secondly, this response is really condescending to the person who is trying to share what they have been through. It basically implies that the person who claims to have seen something unusual is either lying, crazy, or ignorant of what is real and unreal. They are denying those who have encountered ghosts the validity of their experience. And it is usually an experience that has made a deep impact on the person it happened to.

People have different talents and abilities. Some are good at music, some at trading on the stock exchange. I will never be a ballet dancer because I don't have the body, the youth, or the inclination to do so. I will never be an astronaut because I have bad eyesight and an overwhelming fear of small closed-off spaces like space stations. Neither experience will ever be a part of my world that I can experience first hand. But there are people who are experts at performing both tasks, and they do it on an everyday basis. And I can learn about these experiences through the people they happen to because I can listen to their stories of what it was like to experience those things. Some people are good at seeing ghosts and others are not. And those who are live in a world that is very different from those who can't see past the strictly material side of things.

That is not to say that we should believe everyone who claims they have "special powers" to contact and do business with the supernatural, especially those who are marketing those powers for cold hard material cash. And when we hear stories about encounters with the spiritual side of things, we should, of course, first look for a logical explanation for what is going on. When I was a reporter for *Nagoya Avenues* magazine, I once did an article on the city fortunetellers. I interviewed *tei-so* (palm readers), tarot card readers, people that told your fortune by looking at how tea stems floated in your tea cup, people who practice *seimeihandan* (divining your future luck by counting the number of strokes it takes to write the *kanji*

-- the Chinese characters used in Japanese writing --, and some *reibaishi* (channelers or mediums). Almost every one of them was a hustler and a con artist, charging money for putting on a good performance and telling people what they wanted to hear.

But two of the mediums were different. In they first place, they charged no money for what they were doing. In the second place they simply did their thing with no mumbo jumbo show going on, and they told me very specific things about my past that even my best friends didn't know. And yes, I DO know about "cold reading" and how it works. That was not what was going on at the time. You will meet one of these *reibaishi* later in this chapter and you can judge for yourself.

The people presented here, however, are not "fortune tellers". Throughout history and into the present day, there have been people who seem to be more sensitive to the little things that go bump in the night. The people whose stories I am relating here are, for the most part, ordinary people who didn't seek out any supernatural encounters, would rather they never happened in the first place, and certainly have very little to gain from telling other people about what happened. Most are very bothered by what happened and others are merely curious. They tell their stories because it is very human to want to share your life experiences with someone who is sympathetic and willing to listen.

Like many other countries and cultures, the Japanese believe their are certain people who have psychic powers - an ability to see ghosts and other spiritual things that others can not. There is not really any big deal made about this. I have often heard Japanese acquaintances say, "*I don't have the power, but my friend does*", in the same way you might say, "*I'm not so good at tennis, but my buddy can play like crazy*". It's seen as a talent, an accepted part of someone's personality. The term used to describe such people is *reikan ga tsuyoi*, or "he has a strong sensitivity to spiritual things." When they translate it into English, my Japanese friends will often say, "*He has 'an inspiration' to see ghosts.*"

It's not uncommon to be introduced to one of these people and have them say, "*I can see the ghost of your grand mother standing behind you*". Japan's is a culture that was originally based on ancient Shinto and Buddhist ancestor worship. Most homes have a *butsudan,* a shrine to family members who have passed away. It often contains photos of long-gone ancestors, and the family members still living in this world pray at the altar almost every day honoring their ancestors and asking them for help and guidance (although this practice is rapidly declining among the modern youth). It is believed that the dead ancestors can hear such prayers and often hang around the living watching over them and taking care of them.

Like any other talent, there are people who are *reikan ga tsuyoi* in various degrees, from the normal person who sees strange things occasionally to those who define themselves mostly by this ability and who even make a living using this talent. I have met many people in Japan who claim to have seen ghosts at one time or another. I have also met a few who said that they could see all of my ancestors standing behind me watching over me, and there was even one woman who claimed she couldn't drive a car because she was continually seeing so many ghosts that she saw them standing in the road that she was afraid she might swerve to miss them and hit a pedestrian or two. One group of people who make a living using these powers are the before mentioned *reibaishi*, what people in the west would call spiritual mediums or channelers. People often go to them for advice and inspiration.

Here, then are some of the stories of people who are in tune in a special way to the supernatural:

Yoko's Story

This story was originally part of a magazine article I did on local ghost stories for *Nagoya Avenues* magazine back in 1993. Yoko was the first person I ever interviewed who was *reikan ga sugoi*, or able to see ghosts on a regular basis. Yoko's story and my own experiences with ghostly encounters made me eager to meet more of such people, and was the beginning of my quest to seek them out, record their stories, and try to get an understanding of what exactly it is they do and see. It was, and still is, in a way, a search to find a way to validate what I, and some of my friends, have experienced.

Yoko Hayashi is a young woman who lives in Nagoya and comes from an old and prominent samurai family. She has had so many ghostly encounters in her life that she sees them as being a normal part of everyday life. The first happened when she was only five years old. Her older sister had just died a short time before when she woke up one night to see the shadow of a young girl standing at the foot of her bed. Yoko, being perhaps too young to be upset by the apparition, remembers telling the girl in a very matter-of-fact tone, *"I'm sorry, but I'm too tired to play with you right now,"* and then calmly going back to sleep. When she was fifteen, she posed for a photo with her friends during a summer hiking trip to the Norikura ski resort, and the face of a crazed old man appeared reflected in a picture frame behind them when there was no man present in the room.

The spirits of her samurai ancestors seem to still be hanging around the family home. Several times she has heard a swishing sound travel across the floor of her room as if someone wearing *kamishimo* (traditional baggy samurai clothing) were walking around the room. Once she even saw a man in ancient dress standing in her room and staring out of the window. After this she began to experience *kanashibari* in which she would find herself pinned down on her bed and would awake to find a man in full samurai armor sitting on top of her. He would stare into her eyes with a bewildered look on his face as if he were confused or lost. After holding her down for several minutes, he would fade away, leaving her free to move again.

Yoko always relates these tales of her supernatural encounters calmly and with little elaboration. For her, they are merely taken in stride: not much different than the other dramas of daily life.

As part of some of my classes on story telling, I asked my students to interview their friends and family about any ghostly encounters they may have had. Almost all of them were readily able to find someone who could give them a first hand account of a meeting with the supernatural. This first group of stories is from people they found who have experienced the ability to see ghosts.

A Method to Test Your Inspiration

One of the students I interviewed told me about this method young Japanese often use to see if they are *reikan ga tsuyoi* or not:

One day, my friends and I were gathered together at one of their houses and we were telling ghost stories.

One of them said, "We can know if we have the inspiration or not by a certain method. I will teach you this method. First close your eyes and imagine you are standing in your room at home. Look around your room. Then move from room to room in your house, looking around every room in turn. If you meet someone on the way, you have the inspiration."

The next day, one of my friends said, "In fact, I met a man on the way when I imagined my room. The man sat down in my room and glared at me. I was a little surprised. But after I went home, the next day I really saw the man! He sat down in the same place and glared at me!" -- Ikumi Maeda

Yuki's Uncle's Story

This is my uncle's story. This year, in April, my grandmother died. At the wake, my Uncle looked

confused. He turned to me and said, "She is not here. Her soul has gone away somewhere!"

I was surprised at his words. I did not know he had the inspiration to see ghosts before that. At the funeral hall, he was not himself. A priest became concerned, and talked with him. The priest could soon understand that the many ghosts that are around a funeral home bothered my uncle. The priest said a prayer that protected my uncle and he became calm again.

At the funeral, uncle smiled and said, "Now she is back!" I was surprised and glad to hear that. But I couldn't see my grandmother's ghost.

I want to see my grandmother' ghost, but I don't want to see ghosts of people I don't know. I want to talk with my grandmother. I love her very much. I want to say, "I love you, thank you very much for everything."

My uncle can speak with ghosts. I want to do so. I want to speak with my grandmother. This is a true ghost story, but it is not horrible. In this world, there is this type of man like my uncle. At first I didn't believe it, but it is the truth. --Yuki Asano

Misato's Sister

I have never seen ghosts. But my mother and sister have mysterious experiences. My sister doesn't resemble my mother at all, however both of them can see ghosts.

During a Buddhist memorial service for our dead relative at a temple, my sister witnessed something that looked *like a white snake in the room. It crawled up a pillar and gradually disappeared. In Japanese society, it is thought that snakes are the spirits of the house.*

Something else happened during the O-Bon Festival (Japan's festival of the dead. During this time, it is believed the souls of dead ancestors visit the homes of their families, spend time with them for a day and then leave that evening.) At that time there is the custom of "mukae-bi," or "the fire of seeing off our dead ancestors". We light fires so our ancestors can find their way back to heaven and not get lost. At that time, my sister saw two fire balls or "corpse candles" fly away to the sky. --Misato Hayashi

Risa's Friend

When I was a junior high school student, I had a friend who could see ghosts. She said to me, "There are ghosts everywhere, however normal people cannot see them". This is the interesting story she told me:

One day, I slept in my room and I woke up at midnight because I felt a cold wind. The cool wind flowed from the door. I stared at the door and found a man standing in front of the door. His face was pale and his eyes were like gray stone. He said nothing, but he surely looked at me. His gray eyes caught me. I was sure he was a ghost. This is because I sometimes feel wind in my room when the door and window are closed. I think that he is always in the house and I sometimes feel his existence. However, no one in my family except me can see him. But I know ghosts exist in reality. -- Risa Kimura

Daughter and Mother

This is a story that my friend experienced some years ago. At midnight, she suddenly found that she was in front of her apartment. There was no one and no sound, only darkness. Of course, she knew that it was a dream, but it felt so real because the view was too clear for a dream.

When she blinked and opened her eyes, she found herself in bed. Then, a woman who was wearing a white kimono was sitting before her eyes! She looked old, like someone living in the Edo era. The woman stared too close, and my friend could neither move nor close her eyes at all. She knew she was awake and this was real, and she was very afraid of this woman. She tried to call for help, but she couldn't say anything. So she cried, "Mom! Mom, please help me!" in her mind the whole time.

After she had called her mother in her mind many times, her mother came into the room. She said, "In my dream, I heard you call my name!" At that time. The old woman disappeared and my friend could move and speak.

This friend experienced the same thing many times. Whenever she experienced it, she always first dreamed she was in front of her apartment, and then she would awake and meet that woman. Now she believes there is a woman ghost in her apartment. – Yurie Mamiya

The Cursed Family

My friend's family can all see ghosts. And it is common for them to see the ghost of a girl in their house. One day, my friend's father suffered from a serious illness. And soon, on another day, a man attacked his younger sister with a knife. In this way, the family continued to experience unhappiness. Someone who knows about these things told them it was a kind of curse. So, a priest purified them and their house, and their luck changed. They never saw the ghost of the girl again. – Hiroaki Fujisawa

Graduation Ghosts

My friend has the inspiration. During our junior high school graduation ceremony, she saw two boys playing tag on the stage. She wondered why nobody was scolding them and making them stop. Then, they came next to her and smiled at her. She was really surprised. But then, she realized something was strange. She looked over at her friend who also has the inspiration. Her friend nodded. That meant she saw them, too and that the two boys were ghosts. My friend has many stories about the ghosts around her. So I believe in ghosts now. -- Ayumi Yanagigawa

Sekigahara

I live in Tarui Town in Gifu Prefecture. My town is next to Sekigahara Town. We can go there in about ten minutes by car. Sekigahara Town is famous for the Battle of Sekigahara in 1600. This was a very crucial battle in Japan's history. Japan was divided into two groups, the

East Army and the West Army, and they were struggling for all of Japan. This battle only lasted for one day, but many people were killed. So this town is sill famous as a place in which ghosts appear.

I am going to tell you a story, which my mother's friend experienced. She has the inspiration, and she is a very spiritual person. One day when she tried to pass through Sekigahara Town, she suddenly got a very bad headache, and she felt very bad. She couldn't move forward no matter how hard she tried. She could see many samurai who were killed and she could hear the groans of the dying. Since that time, she cannot pass by Sekigahara.

Sekigahara has some places in which many people fought and died, and I have heard of some other spiritual people who also cannot pass there. Especially Sekigahara tunnel is risky. If you have an interest in this story, please come to Sekigahara. -- Wakiko Shimizu

Grandmother's Dreams

My grandmother's dreams make our family frightened. When my father was young, she had a dream. In her dream, her mother (my father's grandmother) came to her house from Nigata Prefecture. She presented several tulips to my grandmother. They later learned that she had died on that day. My father still remembers this because he was very scared at the time.

There is one more thing. The other day, she had another dream. In her dream, her nephew, my cousin, visited the house. A few days later, he was in a serious traffic accident. Fortunately. His life was saved, but he was badly injured. So I want my grandmother to tell me if she has any more strange dreams. -- Mio Matsushita

Teacher's Story

This is a story I heard several years ago from my English teacher. It occurred several years ago with her son who can see ghosts. He always said that there was a boy rummaging through his schoolboy's satchel. But no one else in the family could see the boy. The boy was a ghost and his style of clothing was old, from the Showa Era. In addition to this, her son also often heard footsteps upstairs. No one lived in the upstairs room for a long time, however some of her son's friends who also have inspiration could also hear them.

She did hear a throng of ghosts who went through her apartment once a year. She said it seemed there was a passageway for ghosts going through her apartment. So she had her fortune told and researched the history of her apartment. She found out her apartment building had not had the traditional Buddhist ceremony to drive away evil spirits before it was built. Her family moved. They live in a new house now. But that apartment is still there. -- Mami Taniguchi

Mother's Inspiration

This story is my mother's experience. My mother has had the inspiration since she was young. For example, she often saw ghosts in empty spaces and she had prophetic dreams. These things are not dreadful for her, *but there is one thing that is dreadful: she can recognize the time when someone will die.*

One night, she was washing the dishes and my father was watching TV. The day was normal and peaceful, but, suddenly, she got an awful foreboding. She asked my father to call his father at once, but he said, "I'll do it later", and took a bath. About ten minutes later, the telephone rang. The call was from my grandfather, and he told them that his mother (my great grandmother who lived with them) had just collapsed and had been rushed to the hospital. She was dying when she arrived there and was dead now.

My mother experienced the same feeling when her father died, and I had the same feeling, too. - - Yukiko Saiki

She Has an "Inspiration"

These are stories, which my younger sister's friend has experienced. Since she has an "inspiration", she has seen many things. She realized she had the power when she was little. Her mother also has the inspiration, so she might have inherited it from her mother.

One day when she was still a little girl, she asked her mother, "Who is that girl sitting in the corner of our living room?"

But her mother could not see anyone. Although, when her daughter described the girl, she did not seem harmful, the mother got scared, realizing that her daughter had "the inspiration". So she asked a priest to come and purify the house, and she her bought a lucky charm of protection at a temple. Since that day, my sister's friend has been wearing it so she cannot be possessed by anything bad, but I would like to share some of her stories:

Once, when she was talking on the phone with her friend, she heard loud noises in the background, so she asked her friend, "Is there anyone there besides you? The noise is pretty loud!"

"What are you talking about?" the friend replied. There is only me here in my room."

But my sister's friend could hear another girl in the background, talking loudly and moving around the room. She later learned that the place was supposed to be haunted by the ghost of a girl who had committed suicide in her friend's apartment.

Every time she comes home, from her work place in the dead of night, she sees a woman who has long black hair and is wearing white clothes standing by the side of the road. The woman never does anything, but she is always just standing there.

There is a shrine behind her house. One night she saw a group of little children running around her house and sleeping in the living room. They didn't seem harmful to her, but she was scared anyway. She went to the nearby shrine and asked the priest to come and purify her home.

When he heard her story, the priest nodded as if he knew what she was talking about. "Oh, them," he said.

"Don't worry, they are just playing with you because they know you are scared of them."

They disappeared after the house was purified.

Those are just some of the stories my younger sister' friend shared with me. I had never known there are so many people who have the inspiration in the world until writing this essay. We cannot understand what it is like to be able to see ghosts, but if I were the one who has the inspiration, I would like the people to believe and to listen to me. - - Misaki Sato

She Saw a Pink Teddy Bear

It was early morning on a Saturday in February. The view from my window on the third floor of our apartment building was the same as usual. I heard a door close. I thought my father had left. I was going to wake up, but it was too cold for me to get out of my bed. As I was falling asleep again, my father came back in the apartment and screamed, "A woman is dead!"

I jumped out of bed and went out without changing from my pajamas. There were many people outside and they were still in pajamas, too. Next to our building was a smaller building that held a small hall and the mailboxes for our apartment. That building was two stories tall, so its height was the same as the floor of our third floor apartment. There was a dead woman lying on the roof of that building.

It was very noisy outside with everybody talking at

once, so I went back into our apartment, and into my room. Unfortunately, when I looked out of the window of my room, I could see the scene of the accident. There were police standing there and a man. The man showed no expression, like a zombie. He just continued to look at the dead body in stunned silence.

A tarpaulin covered the dead body. Sometimes the wind blew the tarpaulin up and showed the dead body. She was so bloody I couldn't recognize her face. I wasn't scared at all even though I was looking at a dead body, because I felt like I was watching a horror movie. I watched the scene of the accident from my room for a while, until my mother came in and said, "Stop it!" And then she took me to the living room. After a while, I went back to my room and looked out the window again, but everything was gone. It was just as if nothing had happened. At night, I studied for an hour, and then slept as usual.

The next day, I saw a reporter talking about the incident on TV. She said the woman who had died had two daughters. She had killed one of the daughters. The other had escaped, even though her mother had attacked and injured her. After that, the lady had jumped from the top of our apartment building. I still couldn't feel this had all really happened even though I had seen the body and heard the story on the news.

The next day, I went to school as usual. When I met my friend, she said to me, "I saw the news about the accident. That's really too bad. I was sorry to hear it happened at your place."

"Oh, did you?" I said. "It was terrible!"

Suddenly, she asked me, "By the way, do you happen to have a pink teddy bear?" I had no idea why she would ask me such a thing.

"Yes," I said, "but why?"

She didn't answer my question. But she began asking me about the stuff in my room, especially the stuff on my bed. She correctly told me what my bed looked like, and what kind of stuffed animals I had on my bed, even though she had never been there. I was scared because I had never even told her about my room, or the stuffed animals I had. I nervously asked her, "Why do you know about all this? I have never told you about any of it."

She gave a big sigh and began to talk. "My mother has a friend who has the inspiration," she said. When she was watching the news report on TV, a vision of your room came into her. She had the feeling that something bad would happen around there. She told about it to her friends. My mother was one of them. I heard it had happened at your place, so I thought it might be you."

I didn't understand what she was saying.

"You should tell your parents about it and call her," she said.

After I got home, I told about what my friend had told me to my parents. My mother got scared and began to cry a lot like a child. My father calmed her down. It was the very first time I had seen my mother look afraid.

My father decided to call the spiritualist. While he was talking on the phone, he just nodded. After he had finished, with a serious look on his face, he started to tell us what she had said.

"The woman who died was trying to die together with her family. Her family didn't get along together at home. She died but her ghost is still there. She is gazing at your family with a jealous look from outside. Now your family's bonds are strong so she can't sneak into your house. However, if one of your family should catch a cold, or become weak in any way, then the bond will become weak, and she will sneak into your house and bring on something bad. You should put salt around the window of your daughter's room and place a flower there that is pink or yellow."

Nobody in my family could see the ghost, but we believed the spiritualist. We followed what she said, and kept doing it for two months. I did not sleep in my room again for those two months. After two months had passed. The spiritualist called us.

"You can stop doing it, now," she said. "She has already gone."

Now we are still living happily, and I really appreciate what the spiritualist did, and I appreciate my family's strong bond. -- Shiori Kojima

The following are some first person stories I have collected in interviews with the people who are *reikan ga suyoi*, or, who have the "inspiration" to see ghosts. These are the stories about their experiences in their own words:

Satoko's Story

My mother had the power to know things about people she was close to. She was very close to my grandmother and grandfather - my father's parents, her mother and father-in-law. When my father was young, his mother (my grandmother) decided he needed help in finding a wife. She thought that his wife should be someone who was good with children, so she visited many local kindergartens watching the teachers to see who had a good way with the children. My mother was a young teacher at the time and my grandmother noticed her right away. She saw she was kind and a good worker, so she researched everything about her background and chose her to marry her son.

When they were married, everyone liked each other and my father's parents got an apartment for their son's family and also an apartment for my mother's parents - all close to each other so everyone could see each other often. There were no "in-law" problems at all. Everyone got along very well.

When my grand parents got older, my mother was often over at their house taking care of them. She loved to take care of other people, she had a talent for it, and she always felt close to her mother-in-law because she had chosen her in the beginning.

Then I remember that it was about twenty years ago, one morning in February, around the time of my birthday - it must have been a Sunday because we were all at home, - my mother said she felt really bad, like she had a pain in her heart. That afternoon we got a call from my aunt that my grandmother had had a heart attack that morning and was sent to the hospital. It turned out there was nothing wrong with my mother at all. She was feeling my grand mother's pain. At that time, they didn't do by-pass operations in Japan, and so my grand mother died two weeks later. And my mother was very sad that she was gone. She was so close to her that she had felt her heart pain.

After that my mother was taking care of my grandfather every day at his house because he now lived alone. He had gotten cancer and was not well. Usually she came back home after fixing dinner for my grand father, but one night she called us and said, "I don't feel well. I'm too tired to come back home today."

It was the first time she had ever done this, and my father was worried about her, so my father decided to take the family over to his father's house to have dinner together with my mother there. It was very unusual and I remember my little brother was crying because he didn't want to go. He wanted to eat dinner at home like usual.

We ate dinner and stayed there that night, and that night my grand father died. It was totally unexpected because the doctor had been there that day and said that that day my grand father had eaten a good meal and drank a lot of juice and he seemed stronger. But my mother felt his pain and so my grand father didn't die alone that night. – Satoko ------

A Typical Japanese Ghost Story

This story, told by a friend about her and her family's experiences with the supernatural is especially interesting because it includes many of the most common elements or motifs found repeatedly in such personal narratives in Japan. It includes: the *kanashibari*, or ghost which holds its victim down; the family tradition of being sensitive to ghosts *reikan ga sugoi*; the communication from a relative who has recently died in a far away place; the use of *ofuda* or pieces of paper with a holy Buddhist *sutra* written on it to give protection from unwanted spirits; and the child ghost, which often haunts houses. While these elements appear again and again in the telling of such "true" ghostly encounters, it is rare that all of them will appear in the same story. In this respect, Norie's story can almost be seen as a representative compilation of the Japanese view of how such spiritual experiences are supposed to occur:

Norie's Story

My great grandmother had a strong sense for ghosts. When my mother was a child, she would visit her grandmother and she especially remembered one time when they were in the living room in front of the 'butsudan' (Buddhist altar to dead family ancestors). *Her grandmother said, 'Someone is watching us,' and at that moment, all the candles on the butsudan began to waver and flicker even though there was no breeze.*

My mother also has a very strong sense. When her grandmother (my great grandmother) died, she was living in Kyushu and my mother was in Nagoya. My mother was sleeping. In the middle of the night, she woke up to find her grandmother standing next to her. She told her "Goodbye", and then she was gone. A few hours later, her family got a phone call telling them their grandmother had just passed away.

My mother continued to have the power when she got older. When my family moved to a new house, I was six years old at the time. Almost every night my mother saw a young boy who was walking up and down the stairs. He would walk up and down the stairs and then go out the door. Then the next night he would be there again. My mother was scared, so she went to the temple and got an "ofuda" - a piece of paper with a Buddhist sutra written on I that provides protection from evil. She put it on the stairs, and after that the boy didn't come back.

Ten years later, I started to feel strange at night, as if someone was watching me when I was sleeping. When I closed my eyes, I felt as if someone was there in the room, but when I opened them, no one was there. So I kept the lights on at night because I was scared. For three nights, nothing really happened, so I turned off the light on the fourth night. That night, I had a 'kanashibari.' I fell asleep and then I woke up and felt a strong pressure holding me down. Not like someone holding my body, but a very heavy pressure where I couldn't move even my finger – no part of my body.

I could hear a noise as if it were coming from inside my head -- a deep sound inside my ear. When I opened my eyes, I saw a young boy standing by my bed watching me. It was shaped like a black shadow with eyes in the *shadow: the shadow of a young boy about ten years old. The eyes were watching me. It felt like he was there for a long time, but probably it was only about five minutes.*

I closed my eyes and prayed to every God I knew, "Kamisama, (God) please help me!" Then the boy was gone, and I could move.

The next day I told my mother about it and she told me about the boy she had seen on the stairs ten years before. My mother also told me she had noticed that the 'ofuda' had gotten worn out and had fallen off the wall three days ago. She had gone to the temple and bought a new one, but hadn't gotten around to putting it up yet. She out it up and the boy never came back again, but every time we go near the stairs, we get a strange feeling. Even my brother doesn't like going on the stairs. -- Norie Oba

Norie's Story Part II

Norie works at the same university I do, although not in the same department, so I don't meet her all that often. About three years after Norie told me the story about the ghost of the little boy, I happened to run into her as she was on her way to a meeting. We had a short chat, and she told me she had recently had yet another encounter with a ghostly being. I immediately set up an appointment for an interview, and over lunch, she related the following story to me:

I knew I had the sense to detect the presence of ghosts. My mother has it stronger than I, but I hadn't seen anything since high school, so I thought maybe my sense was getting weaker and weaker, and maybe it was gone. I

really hoped so, because I didn't want to see any more of that type of thing.

This last summer I moved from my parent's home to my own apartment in the Jiyugaoka area of Nagoya. I was enjoying living alone, but I sometimes had a strange feeling as if someone was watching me. Then one night, I got up in the middle of the night to go to the toilet. My apartment is my bedroom, which is connected to my dining room. Beyond the dining room is a long hall to the toilet and then the door leading out of the apartment.

I went though the dining room in the dark and then opened the door to the hallway. I was surprised to see a white shape standing in the hallway. I thought someone was there in front of me. It looked like white smoke in the shape of a man. I couldn't see any face or features, but it was clearly in the shape of a human.

Then the white smoke came toward me, coming though the door into the dining room, into the area where I lived. It passed right by me, so close that it was about to touch my shoulder! I realized it was a ghost and I screamed.

The ghost stopped and reacted like it was surprised, too. It seemed like it wasn't aware that I could see it. Its reaction was like it was surprised and saying, "Oh! You can see me!" Then it moved back away from me and disappeared. It didn't come into the dining room, the place where I live.

When I was young, I had seen ghosts many times, so we always had protection put up around our house: the holy "ofuda" papers from the temple to keep away evil. I hadn't seen any ghosts for a long time, so when I moved into my own apartment, I thought I didn't need any protection. Maybe that's why the ghost was able to come.

The next day, I went back to my parent's house to get my protection, the "ofuda" papers I had left there. When my mother asked why I wanted them, I told her. I got them and brought them to my apartment. I put them up to protect me. I didn't se the ghost again, but for a month after that, I could still feel that he was there in the hallway. I ran quickly to the toilet when I had to go at night. Then, after a month, I knew he was gone.

Since then, I sometimes feel there is something else there, but I have seen nothing. My apartment is by a graveyard; maybe that is where the ghost came from. Also, at the time I saw it, I was very busy at work. My boss was really nasty and I was feeling tired and weak: very stressed. Maybe that is why I saw it. It came because I was too weak to keep it away. Now I have a new boss who is nice and I feel much stronger. Maybe when I am strong I won't see them. I thought my sense to see ghosts was gone and I hope it will go away. I don't want to see them any more. – -Norie Oba

Mai's Many Ghosts

When I asked some of my students to tell about any encounters they might have had that were in the realm of the supernatural, one of my students named Mai told me this very interesting story.

My family is composed of five people, but another three

people live in my house. Of course these people aren't human. They are ghosts. All of them are men. One person is what we call a "fleeing samurai". His face looks very fierce and he has many arrows in his back. He always sits in the same place. Another person is also a soldier but I don't think he is a fleeing samurai. He is wearing red and black armor, and he is riding on a horse. He always runs about on his horse. And the last person, he is a child. He was a child, maybe, during wartime in World War 2. His hair is close cropped, and he is wearing a beige T-shirt and pants. Sometimes he waves to me. They are not scary. They only stay in the same place. They are also my family!

I went to Mai and asked her if she would consent to a more extended interview about her experiences seeing ghosts and she quickly agreed. During the interview, she was quite relaxed and open about sharing her life history with the spiritual. I soon came to realize that she was a classic example of *reikan ga suyoi*: a special individual who can easily see into the nether world of ghostly beings and who sees them on a regular basis. While she was quite disturbed by some of her first encounters of this type when she was younger, she has come to accept meetings with the otherworldly as a natural and normal part of her life. Her friends also are well aware of her special talents and accept them as part of who she is and what she does. Her then, in her own words, is Mai's story:

The first time I saw a ghost I was twelve. My grand father had just died. A few weeks later I saw him sitting on the floor reading the paper. It was a summer afternoon, or maybe early September? It seemed very natural for him to be there, so I was maybe more surprised than scared. I saw him circle the day's winning lottery numbers with a pen. He slowly disappeared, but the pen and the paper were still there. I looked at the paper, but lottery numbers were not circled. He liked to play the lottery when he was alive and always checked the winning numbers every day.

The second time I was on the first floor of our house, which was a sushi bar. My parents owned the bar. We lived in the apartment on the second floor. I was sitting in the sushi restaurant studying my homework, and grandpa walked by. I only saw his legs clearly. He walked outside. It was clearly his pants and his shoes I saw. At that time of day, he always went outside and walked around the neighborhood. It was walk time.

After that second time, I told my family about it. My grandmother was excited an anted to see him, but she couldn't, so she was sad. She was sad about that, but she did see him in her dream later.

The third time I saw him, I had gone to bed. I wanted to sleep, but then his shadow came by. I could see it on the "shoji". (traditional wall made of thin translucent white paper). He was outside my room. He walked past my room and into the next room, which was the "butsuma". It had the "butsudan". (The butsuma is the room where the Buddhist altar (butsudan) to honor then family's dead ancestors is kept).

My aunt is also "reikan ga tsuyoi". She lived in Osaka for a while, and one day she got on a train. The train stopped at a station in front of a big department store. As she got off the train, she saw a man fall from the roof of the department store onto the street. A suicide. Just before he hit, he made eye contact with her. He hit by her and he hit so hard, his head was missing. She said, "Oh, no, he has no head!" She helped them look for his head.

After that she could see the three ghosts in our house.

My aunt works in a clothes boutique. When she was working there one day, a man got on the elevator with her. His face was very white and blue. There was a scary air around him. He pushed the button for the fifth floor, but the fifth floor was not being used at that time. She felt scared, so she pushed the button for the third floor, but the elevator didn't stop at the third floor, it went on to the fifth and the man got out. Later she asked her boss, "Did anything strange happen on the fifth floor?"

Her boss told her someone had committed suicide on the fifth floor by hanging himself. My aunt's co-workers never saw the man, but they said sometimes the fifth floor lights went on and off, but no one was using that floor.

There are three ghosts in our house. One is a young boy with a shaved head. He is wearing a brown shirt and pants, so maybe he lived during the time of World War Two. He is very thin. But he is not scary. Sometimes he waves to smiles and me. I see him in front of the big mirror in the "genkan" (entrance hall to the house), (entrance hall to the house).

The other is an old man. What we call an "ochimushya". A soldier defeated in battle. He always has a scary face and looks very angry. He is always sitting, leaning forward with his elbows on his knees. He sits at the end of the hallway. He is wearing samurai armor. His back has many arrows sticking out of it. When I was a child, I saw him for the first time. Only his eyes move to look at me. The first time I saw him, I shouted, "Get Out!" But he was still there, so I ran away. So now I don't go to the end of the hallway if I can help it.

The third ghost is a samurai on a horse. He rides around my father's room on the second floor. My father doesn't see it. That room is sitting between two tombs that are outside the house. The samurai rides between the two tombs, through the room and out through the wall. Our town is a castle town. "Kaumbei-jo", or Kaumbei Castle is there. Sometimes there were battles in the area, so maybe many samurai died near my house. My father said that, when I was three or four, I used to go into his room. I would look at the ceiling and laugh and clap my hands, so maybe I saw him then.

When I was in elementary school, maybe I was about twelve, my family went to Okinawa. On our trip we visited "Hemeiyuri No Tou" a famous cave where people hid and died in World War Two. This was the first time I ever got a very scary feeling. There is a museum there. They have clothing, medical supplies the nurses used, like hypodermic syringes, and guns. The smell is like medicine or a hospital. The cave also smells bad, like mud. My nose is very sensitive, so I didn't like the smell.

I went alone into the next room, and I felt very tired. That room was near an old air raid shelter. The moment I saw it, I felt someone grab my arms and try to pull me down into the shelter. It was a very strong power. There was a rope barrier there. I grabbed the rope and pulled myself back. So I wasn't pulled into the shelter. It was very scary. I was very surprised. I ran away from that room. I couldn't stay in that museum, so I went outside and waited alone for my family. I was very scared.

When I told my family about it, they believed me. They knew my aunt could see ghosts, so they figured I was the same as my aunt.

When I was in junior high school, we made a class trip to Hiroshima. Before we went, I didn't want to go near the "Genbaku Dome" (Atomic Bomb Dome), or the "Genbaku Museum (Atomic Bomb Museum)". Or the bridge there, it's famous, but I can't remember the name right now. (She might be referring to the Aioi Bridge, which was near the bomb detonation site).

The bus went to Hiroshima City. Suddenly I felt very bad, tired, and weak. I had a bad headache. First we went to the Dome. I only looked at it from a distance because I felt so bad. My classmates were laughing and having fun. They took a class picture in front of the Dome, and I thought it was crazy. In the photo, my face looks very serious and tired in the picture.

Next we went to the Peace Statue, and then to the bridge. When I walked on the bridge, I felt many, many, sad feelings come into my heart. I began to cry. My tears came and they wouldn't stop. I didn't want to cry, but something came into e and I couldn't stay there. My friends asked, "Why, what's wrong?" I said, it's not MY feelings, but I can't stop crying.

That bridge is a famous place. The atomic bomb created a firestorm. Many people were burned, and ran into the river to escape. But the river was boiling and many people died in the river. When I saw the river and the water, I could feel that so many people had died there. I felt the spectacle of their death drama. And so I cried.

Next we went to the museum, but I couldn't go in. My teacher stayed with me and took me far away from the museum. We talked and waited for the class to return.

When I was in high school, one day I was in biology class. I was sitting by the door. I heard some footsteps outside in the hall. But this was class time and I thought it was strange because no one should be there. I thought maybe some student was gong to see the school nurse.

The steps came closer to the classroom. I saw someone with yellow-green eyes looking at me through the small window in the door. The door was a little ajar. Something that looked like a big cloud of green gas with two yellow eyes came into the room. It was standing in front of my desk and looking at me. It was maybe only two minutes, but it seemed like a very long time. I was trying to avoid looking at it, looking down at my desk, but when I looked up, it was still there. I kept thinking, "Please get out! Please get out!"

Suddenly the gas disappeared, but I felt it had broken up into scary smaller particles of gas, which spread all over the room. So I screamed, "Please open the window!" My classmates knew I could see ghosts, so they opened the window.

I left the classroom and went to the nurse's room. I wanted to rest, but the nurse's room had a ghost, a young girl about my age with long wavy permed hair. I cold see her face clearly. While I was lying on the bed, she touched me and moved the curtain, preventing me from sleeping. She was teasing me, making fun of me. Not dangerous, but mischievous.

While I was staying there, a girl came into the room that had broken her leg. Then the ghost went over by her. After that I got a bad feeling that the ghost was always there and that she was attracted to the sick and injured girls who came there. After that, I didn't see her, so maybe she followed the other girl when she was taken out.

I told my aunt about the green gas, and she said there is something called an "animus" that stays in the world. Humans have many feelings. An animus is a very simple feeling; it's not a person. It stays around for about a year after you die.

Nowadays when I ride the train I see three ghosts at Miyamado station. There is usually no one there at the station and there are four seats there. I can see three shadows in the chairs. The station is near a big Shinto shrine. Behind the station is a very big "tori" gate to the shrine. So maybe there are ghosts there. – Mai Miyazaki

Note: Mai was my student at the university when I interviewed her. Shortly after the interview, my family and I were eating at a *yaki niku* (grilled meat) restaurant one night with friends. One friend asked about how my progress on "the ghost book" was going, and I told the group about my recent interview with Mai. We left the restaurant, and the discussion continued as we walked down the street. Several blocks later, just as we passed by, who should emerge from a busy café, but Mai and two of her friends.

"*Oh!*" she said. "*This is the professor I've been telling you about. He sees ghosts, too.*"

While I was telling her story, she had been talking about me, and in some weird manifestation of synchronicity, we came together at that exact moment in the middle of busy downtown Nagoya. She greeted me with a happy expression on her face, I greeted her back, and every one else stood there looking stunned. She told me later that her two friends were particularly weirded-out by that meeting, and they never quite reacted to her in the same way afterwards. Mai, however, had the attitude of, "*Of course! We are both reikan ga tsuyoi. So of course we have a connection and were brought together.*" And, to tell the truth, I am inclined to agree with her.

Ms. M and the Sixth Sense Ghostbusters

(Note: the lady whose life was involved in the following events asked that her real name not be used, so she will be referred to as "M" in this essay).

M has struggled with her sensitivity to the spiritual world almost her entire life. It began at about the age of eight. When she went to bed each evening, the sheets on her bed would move up and down as if something were underneath them like a mouse or small animal. She would hit them to smooth them down and make them stay still before she went to sleep. The whole process took about five minutes every night and she wasn't bothered by it because she thought it was normal. She never compared experiences with anyone else, so she thought everyone experienced it.

She experienced her first *kanashibari* at about this time as well. She was sleeping one night and her heart started pounding so fast that she woke up. Her heart was beating faster and faster and she found she couldn't move any part of her body except her eyes. Then she felt something approaching her in the room. Her eyes were locked on the ceiling, but she could see around her in what she describes as "panorama style". She first sensed and then saw a "gray man" standing next to her. His face had no features; he was more like a shadow. He talked to her in a *hikui* (deep low voice), but she couldn't understand what he was saying. He was there for one or two minutes and then he was gone. After he left, she fell off to sleep again, but she says, "*I know it wasn't a dream. It was real.*" After that, the same thing continued to happen to her once or twice a week for some time. Later these events would get more involved and the gray man would come to her, sit on her chest, strangle her, pull her leg, and do other things to bother her. She never felt it was trying to kill her or really harm her, just scare her. "*It would sometimes come to me two or three times in one night,*" she says. "*The next day I would be very tired and my body would feel very heavy.*"

This happened continually until she was twelve or so. Then she wanted to find a way to avoid the *kanashibari*. "*This is menrokusai,*" (bothersome) she thought. She wanted to have a peaceful night's sleep. To stop it, she soon learned that when her heart first began to pound, there was a certain space of time when she could still move her body. If she suddenly jerked her shoulder and moved her body, the *kanashibari* would immediately stop. "*It was the same as when I was married and my husband wanted sex when I was tired*", she laughs when telling the story. "*I would jerk away, saying, 'No!' and he would desist coming at me.*"

She soon realized the *kanashibari* wanted something from her. When she was a child, she didn't understand, but now she knows it wanted her attention. It wanted to say, "*I am here! Look at me!*"

These occurrences had a strange effect on her mentally. She became bulimic. "*I don't know why I did it. I was like a wild animal. I couldn't stop eating. I would eat a whole plate of cooked meat, would even eat the meat half raw if it wasn't cooked fast enough.*" And then she would force herself to regurgitate it later. The *kanashibari* was still trying to come to her and she didn't know how to make it stop annoying her. She didn't realize then that it had to do with her sensitivity to the supernatural.

She tried to talk to her parents and others around her about this problem, but they acted as if she were having mental problems. They were unable to help her or explain to her what was happening.

This problem continued until a few years ago when she was introduced to a group that calls itself "The Sixth Sense" The only way I can describe this organization is that it is a support group for people in Japan who have been plagued by spirits and the supernatural. They give each other information about what the spirit world is. They teach those in trouble how to protect themselves from supernatural attacks and even how to exorcise a persistent ghost if need be. Most importantly, they let each other know that they are not alone, and not crazy, but are experiencing something many other people have had to deal with as well. And they teach each other how to do something about the problem to make the situation better. Using their advice and training, M was soon able to protect herself from her nightly terrors and to prevent them from happening again.

When M heard that I had had several experiences with the supernatural and that I was doing research into such otherworldly areas, she told me she was worried about my safety. She gave me a special *omamori* or amulet that she had spent a long time praying over to protect me and invited me to meet the leader of The Sixth Sense group, Ishikawa-sensei.

I first met Ishikawa-sensei in a hotel room in Tokyo where he was conducting meetings and interviews with people who needed his help. He was a well-built man in his forties or early fifties, who spoke softly, smiled and laughed a lot, but had an aura of quiet strength around him. Another younger man who was in training to develop the expertise and techniques that Ishikawa-sensei had to teach attended him. Both were wearing the blouse-like shirts and *hakuma* style skirts that are usually associated with *kendo* sword fighting or Japanese martial arts. He was very congenial to talk to and seemed very interested in hearing about an American's experiences with and interest in the supernatural. He was not very forthcoming when asked how he attained his knowledge of how to deal with visitations from things that are not of this world, stating only that he had had many encounters with ghostly spirits himself and he was inspired to figure it out for himself. Now he wished to help others and use his abilities to stop the suffering of the people who came to him. To tell the truth, while he was very humorous and pleasant to talk to, I went away not really much more informed with what he was all about than when I went in. There was no great philosophy or insight he had to pass on, just a practical working knowledge of the existence of the types of spirits that bother people and how to deal with them.

The important word here is "practical". What the Sixth Sense group does is present a practical way to help haunted people who are bedeviled by spirits. Ms. M drew me a very complicated diagram of the spiritual universe as Ishikawa-sensei and the Sixth Sense people see it, and most of the explanation was pretty hard to follow. The basic concepts that were presented were: (1) there is a spirit world different than the one most people are cognizant of; (2) it's filled with several different types of spirits that can interact with us under certain circumstances; (4) we have souls that live on after we die and they can interact with us as well; and; (5) a lot of the ways these various spirits interact with us have to do with karma or the results of the cause and effect of what we and the people around us do. There is nothing very new or really all that enlightening here. The important message that Ishikawa-sensei had to impart was a simple one that said, "*If you are being bothered by supernatural phenomena, I believe you and I can help*".

This simple message, however, seems to be what most of the members of the Sixth Sense group need to hear. I was invited to a special dinner party held by the Sixth Sense group in Nagoya. It was held on Halloween night (of course!). We met at a traditional Japanese restaurant and there were about 40 people in attendance, most of them women. Ishikawa-sensei was there and his male acolyte dressed in their traditional garb. I was seated at the head table close to Ishikawa-sensei with a lady who spoke fluent English as my interpreter. While we ate, one lady was playing a strange bamboo reed-pipe type of instrument that made eerie sounds to set the mood for a Halloween dinner spent among a society of ghost busters.

During the course of the meal, several of the ladies, especially those who spoke English, came up to me to talk about their experiences with the supernatural. Most of the stories were very similar: They had been plagued with ghostly visitations from an early age. When they tried to tell their parents, family, or friends about it, they were

141

judged to be crazy, and some of them had even spent time in mental hospitals for no other reason than that they insisted they could see ghosts on a regular basis. Then they discovered the Sixth Sense group: their claims and, ultimately their sanity were validated. They learned that they weren't alone, that they weren't crazy, just sensitive to things that most other people were not. Some of them were even carrying "before and after" photos showing how harassed and depressed they looked before they joined the group, and how happy and strong they looked now. And, indeed the dinner party was full of what looked like well adjusted, smiling people enjoying a good meal.

So what am I to think about all of this? It's true that Ishikawa is making a living off of this group. There is a hefty initial charge for the amulet that protects you from supernatural attacks, and a small fee is required to be sent in each month for the sensei to keep praying for you and to keep it active. The amulet is in a pouch you wear around your neck and I was told it contained a cutting from a peach tree among other things. It's the sacred prayers that are said over it that give it its power as a blessed object. He charges a fee for the consultations when people come to see him at the hotels. I don't know what he charges for visiting your house and exorcising the spirits there. I saw no evidence of anyone being financially devastated by demands for money in the way many cults operate.

In addition, while I am very suspicious of any group that centers itself around the power of one individual (especially when most of the members are women), I saw no glassy-eyed zombies spouting fanatic rhetoric or undying devotion to the great leader as would be expected from a mind-controlling religious group. The members simply seemed very grateful that they had been helped, and had found a community of people with whom they could share their common experiences.

It appeared that there was definitely some very effective therapy going on here.

People, who once felt damaged, depressed and shunned, now felt accepted and understood. And those who once felt vulnerable to events they couldn't control now felt protected and safe. This was an unusual community of individuals, to say the least, but the Sixth Sense group didn't control them as some religious organizations try to do; everyone had their own personal lives going on and they seemed to be doing okay at them.

Best of all, from my point of view, they all listened to my stories of ghostly encounters and believed every word, even nodded and said, "*Yes! I know exactly what you are talking about.*" They all offered to be available for my phone call should I ever again be bothered by supernatural events of any kind. I declined the offer to join the group, but I walked away glad I had met them.

(Note: During the time when I was corresponding with and meeting Ms. M. for interviews, I had a somewhat unsettling encounter with a ghostly presence of my own. At the time, I was dating a Japanese lady let's call her "K.", who on the surface seemed like a lovely lady. She was intelligent and full of fun, and did a lot of work for charities and volunteer organizations, which led everyone to believe she had a kind and benevolent character.

One evening, however, after a romantic dinner, K. stayed over at my place. We were sleeping in my big Queen-sized bed, with K. lying next to the wall, and I was sleeping on the side of the bed that was open to the rest of the bedroom. As she slept, K. suddenly began screaming in her sleep, a blood curdling sound straight out of a horror movie as if she was having the most terrible nightmare of all time. At the same time that she started screaming, a loud stomping sound began on the floor next to where I was sleeping, as if someone very big and massive was tromping back and forth beside the bed in heavy leather boots. I sat up, almost deafened by the sound of K.'s screaming coming in one ear and the loud thuds pounding up and down the floor in the other. I looked directly at the floor beside my bed and there was nothing there that could be seen, but I could very much feel the hulking presence next to me and the whole bed was shaking to the vibrations of its walloping steps on the floor.

I woke up K., and the sound of the foot stompings stopped immediately. I asked K. if she were okay, if she was having a nightmare. She said, no she wasn't having any kind of dream at all, and asked why did I wake her up? I explained that she had been screaming in her sleep and sounded as if she were in trouble. "*No*", she said, "*I wasn't screaming and I wasn't dreaming*", and she promptly fell back to sleep.

As soon as she fell back to sleep, she began screaming again as if she were being murdered, and whatever was marching next to me began pounding the floorboards again as loudly as before. I woke her up again and once again, she denied either screaming or dreaming. She looked annoyed, turned over and fell asleep again. And the foot stomping walked up and down the room next to me just as they had before.

I would like to point out several things about this occurrence, all of which still puzzle me to this day:

1. The two phenomena were definitely connected. The foot stompings only occurred while K. was asleep and screaming. As soon as she was awakened, they immediately stopped. And they did not occur again until she had fallen back to sleep and began once more to scream.

2. I was not asleep or dreaming when I heard all this, neither was I imagining any if it. Five times in a row, I sat straight up in bed stared at K. as she screamed, and looked intently at the floor as the heavy feet pounded on the wooden floorboards next to the bed.

3. This happened at least five times within a very short period. Four times I awakened K. out of her screaming sleep to ask if she were all right. Four times the boots stopped at the same time. Four times K. denied there was anything wrong. The fifth time, I just let her scream and, strangely unafraid by this time, went with the experience as the feet marched next to me, and after a few minutes, K. began to sleep peacefully and whatever had been goose stepping next to me stopped. Eventually I fell asleep as well. In the morning K. asked me why I had rudely bothered her sleep so many times, and when I told her what had happened, she didn't say anything, but she did not look very surprised.

4.   The creature tromping next to me gave me the feeling rather like some kind of predatory beast (albeit in boots and walking on two legs), that was very displeased at my being with K. and I am sure that the performance was some kind of warning directed at me. Curiously, however, I felt more startled than frightened throughout the whole performance, and never felt in danger of anything more than losing a good night's sleep.

5. And the most amazing thing of all to me was that the next morning after K. had left, I received a phone call from Ms. M. of the Sixth Sense group asking if I was all right. She said she knew I had had some kind of encounter, she could sense it, and was worried about me.

Needles to say, K., and I broke up shortly after that. For several reasons, not worth relating here, I later learned she had had a very troubled past, a combination of perceived unkindness's from others along with some mental problems and bad life choices. We remain friends to this day, but I still worry about her. There is an inner core of real sweetness and generosity in the lady, and I hope she works out her "personal demons" in some way that will bring her a happy and fulfilled life.

Keeping the Spirits Happy:

An Interview With a Buddhist Faith Healer

Early in my search for people with special powers that kept them in touch with the supernatural side of things, I came across Mr. Nakane, the Japanese version of what we would call a charismatic "faith healer" back in the America. Two Japanese co-workers who went to him for help because of the special abilities he possessed introduced me to him. What followed was a tale of ghostly hauntings and miracle healings. This article first appeared in *Nagoya Avenues* magazine for which I was a reporter and editor at the time. This story opened my eyes to a very Japanese way of thinking about the spiritual, the ghostly, and the religious.

I learned a long time ago that it is possible for to people to be in the same room at the same time, and yet be living in two entirely different worlds. However, every so often I encounter a situation in which the point is driven home with such force that the boundaries of my own frame of reference get shaken a bit, and moved to one side or the other, in order to at least attempt to encompass part of the world inhabited by the fellow standing next to me. My interview with Fujio Nakane was just such an instance.

I find it difficult to comment on or analyze what was said and done. Nakane espouses a belief system that is pretty alien to the modern Western mind. What he believes in is based on a kind of pantheistic-shamanic-Shinto-Buddhist folk religion which, when I look at it objectively, is really not so different from some of the more far-out charismatic Christian faith-healers I saw so often back home in Indiana in the USA. The best I can do, dear readers, is simply to relate what I was told and what I saw, and let you do with it what you will.

I was introduced to Mr. Nakane by a friend who prefers to remain anonymous, so let's just all her Ako (not her real name, of course). Ako is a young Japanese woman, married, with two children. Last spring, Ako and her family were given a present from her husband's parents. Her in-laws enjoy collecting valuable antiques, and the gift they presented Ako's family with was a beautiful antique vase from China. Ako and her family thanked their benefactors, and placed the vase on prominent display in their home.

Soon Ako's young daughter began having nightmares. In the most disturbing one, she saw twelve women in white kimono-like dresses (the kind put on the dead during funeral ceremonies), float above the vase and come to the foot of her bed. The nightmares became so frequent that Ako decided she must do something to help her daughter. She heard through a friend about a man in Gamagori City who could help with such things, and she went to meet him. Thus, she was introduced to Mr. Fujio Nakane.

According to Ako, all she told Mr. Nakane was that she had received a vase, and asked if it was a good thing to keep it. No mention was made of her daughter's dreams.

After meditating on the problem, and without ever seeing the vase, Nakane told her that the vase was of the type that had been used to inter the bones of the dead in cemeteries in ancient China. The twelve women—possibly a noble woman and her servant ladies—whose bones it had once held haunted it. She should get rid of it a soon as possible. Ako was impressed by Mr. Nakano's ability to describe what had been in her daughter's dreams so exactly without being told about the dreams at all.

Ako refrained from telling her husband anything about any of this—the vase, her daughter's nightmares, the meeting with Mr. Nakane—because he believes in nothing that is out of the ordinary and refuses to talk about anything that is. Instead, she did a little research on her own. Going to the library, she pored over books of ancient Chinese art until she found a picture of a vase almost exactly like the one she had been given. And, sure enough, it was a funereal vase, in which the Chinese used to place the bones of the dead. Ako gave the vase back to her in-laws, stating that she was afraid to keep such a valuable object in the house because her children might break it while playing.

That same evening after she had returned the vase, Ako was awakened from sleep by her husband's shout. He told her he had just had a frightening dream in which a woman in a white kimono appeared to him in his mother's garden. According to Ako, however, from that moment on, there were no more strange nightmares in her household. Dear readers, I don't ask you to believe any of this, I only relate it to you as it was told to me.

I was told another story by a woman I shall call Akemi

(again, not her real name). Akemi had injured her left shoulder in such a way that it was always dislocating itself from its socket, a total of eight times by her count. Twice it happened in front of one of her friends who said, "*Akemi, I can see a white hand on your shoulder!*"

Not knowing what to make of this, Akemi went to Mr. Nakane, who told her that the ghost of one of her dead ancestors was bedeviling her. He performed a ritual and said a prayer to send the troubled soul to its rest, and Akemi swears she has never had trouble with her shoulder since.

I met Mr. Nakane in his place in Gamagori City. His home is in Anjo City, but he receives people in a special room in Gamagori every night from 7:00 PM to 11:00 PM. It is a hard room to describe. It's been turned into a kind of private shrine with Shinto drum, Buddhist altar, and various religious statues and icons scattered about. Mistakenly supposing I was in a temple, I asked him what religious sect he was a member of. He replied, "*This is not a temple. Many Gods come together in this place.*"

He introduced me to his partner, a lady named Shiyonin Suzuki. "*The Gods come into her body,*" he explained. "*Through her, I can learn what to do.*"

Realizing at this point that this was not going to be your usual reporter-on-the-street interview, I sat back and let things take their own course. Mr. Nakane proceeded to give me a brief history of how he had received his miraculous powers. To understand the mood that prevailed throughout the interview, you have to imagine the phone ringing every ten minutes or so with people on the other end asking for advice and guidance.

Also, various neighbors dropped by now and then, singly or whole families at a time. Some of the questions put to him by the phone-ins included, "When is a good time to sell my business?" and, "*What time is auspicious to begin building my new home?*" After each inquiry, Mr. Nakane would break off the conversation; make a sudden downward chopping motion with his hand, and shout, "*Eh!*" We would then meditate for about ten seconds before he shouted out his answer to the caller's question, and then he would pick up our conversation again at the exact point he had left off.

One lady phoned in to say, "*I was chanting a Buddhist sutra and suddenly I began crying and I can't stop. What does it mean?*"

"*You have made a dead spirit happy and it is expressing its gratitude through your body,*" he replied.

"*Oh!*" exclaimed one of the women present in the room. "*The same thing happened to me not long ago!*"

Mr. Nakane's journey into mysticism began when he was fifty years old. He had worked hard to make a successful business—he owned a factory that manufactured metal looms used for industrial weaving. Each day he would visit a temple in Anjo City to give thanks for his good fortune.

One day, after about two years of daily prayers of gratitude, as he faced a statue of Buddha, he heard a voice say, "*Help the world, help the people!*" At first he was very confused by this, but he continued to hear a voice "like electricity or light" in his mind. Then a vision of the goddess Sai-Shi-Hanna-Himme-No-Okame appeared before him and told him she would send a woman to help him in his mission.

Later, he attended a *bonenkai* (end of the year party), and he met Seiko Suzuki. He was immediately drawn to her because her face was the same as the goddess who had appeared before him. After much convincing, she agreed to help him, and together they began to visit Shinto shrines all over Japan to ask for instruction. Working together with Ms. Suzuki, it took Nakane seven years to acquire the powers and the knowledge he needed to help others. During this time, a succession of deities appeared before him, each one bestowing a specific power or blessing upon him.

He was convinced his search was over, when another *Bosatsu* appeared and told him to go to a hill in Miyazaki, where a water god was supposed to live, and to pray. "A treasure will be given unto you," he was promised. While he and Ms. Suzuki were praying on the hill, a waterfall suddenly sprang up from a spring in the ground above them, and began falling at their feet. Nakane always keeps a jug of water from this waterfall, which he offers to visitors to ensure good health. It tastes like mineral spring water, and is very refreshing.

After this last event, Nakane and Suzuki have worked together to help others. When someone comes to them with a problem, they sit close together and meditate. According to them, Suzuki (who is now known by the name of *Shiyonin*, or "Saint") is like a cosmic lightening rod; the gods send the power through her, and she sends it on to Nakane, who uses this power to find the answer to the problem that is before them. On the fifteenth of every month, they hold a ceremony in which people gather and Suzuki sends power to them from the gods to give the people strength and mercy.

No matter how hard it is for the Western mind, or even most Japanese to believe all of this, you must understand what high esteem the local people hold Nakane and Suzuki. During the interview, whole families from the neighborhood would drop by to give testimonials on how the pair had helped them in business, with personal troubles, and in healing their personal maladies.

One family named Ishiguro told how the two mystics had quickly healed their daughter who had severely injured her eye while playing with a pair of scissors. Nakane told them that the injury had occurred because they had cut down a huge camphor tree in their yard without apologizing to the spirit in the tree (an obvious continuance of some very old Shinto folk beliefs). Mrs. Ishiguro placed a statue of *Kannon-sama* (the Buddhist Goddess of Mercy), before the stump and prayed, and the child's eye was soon out of danger and quickly healed.

Another family told me that their son's wife became depressed and weak, her face breaking out with a rash. Nakane told her that the spirit of her baby who had been stillborn was unhappy; it had badly wanted to live. According to the family they were astonished, as they had not told Mr. Nakane that the daughter-in-law had lost a child. They followed his instructions to "pray and try to understand the feelings of the baby". They chanted a sutra called the *Hannya Shinkyoo*, and the daughter-in-law soon became strong and happy.

So, how do we describe Mr. Nakane and his partner Ms. Suzuki? Are they charlatans bilking their neighbors with a good line of patter or an entertaining show? According to the people I talked to, Nakane usually doesn't take any money for his services; he's already rich and doesn't need it. So why does he do what he does? To feel self-important? Does he really believe in what he says?

Perhaps what is most important is that the people who come to him believe in him. This interview provided me with a really close-up look at a very old form of folk religion and belief system. Mrs. Ishiguro told me she comes to Nakane because he provides very direct answers to their problems. "*He tells us specifically what the cause of our problems are, and how we can take action ourselves to solve them.*"

According to Nakane, unhappy spirits of the dead who cannot enter reikai, or the spirit world causes almost every problem in life. Thus, they are wandering, lost, and confused, and sometimes create problems for the living. His job is to primarily help these suffering spirits, and, by doing so, to help the living as well.

Sitting in the room, among Mr. Nakane, Ms. Suzuki and their friends, I tried to imagine a world in which a host of dead spirits floated constantly around me, causing me happiness or harm. I find it difficult to imagine. But then, I once tried to describe sixties rock music to a group of fishermen living on a small island in the middle of the Philippines where there was no electricity or TV. I don't think they believed a word I said, either.

Mr. Nakane told me that the spirit of my mother's mother is always with me, guarding and protecting me. It happens to be true that I was Grandma's favorite grandchild, and she did her best to spoil me rotten. I am sure that, although if the old girl were watching, there would be many things of which she would not approve, I find the thought that she might be hanging around rather comforting. Thanks, grandma, and keep up the good work.

Visits by Relatives: Loved Ones Come Calling

One of the most prevalent types of story collected was that of a visit by a recently deceased relative or loved one. The purpose of these visitations seems to be to announce their recent death and say farewell, since, very often, the person being visited is unaware that the person visiting had died. Usually the news of the loved one's death comes later or the next day. This type of experience is generally accepted as real among the Japanese, as it is very much in keeping with their culture's ideas about the closeness of the family and its ancestors who have passed on.

As with many other cultures, Japanese traditional thinking includes the belief that dead ancestors should not only be respected and venerated, but that they still remain a very active and involved part of the family. A traditional Japanese house has a room with a *butsudan*, or Buddhist altar honoring the family dead. The *butsudan* has pictures of relatives who have passed on, where candles are lit, incense burned, and daily prayers are offered up for their well being and happiness. Often food, drinks, or even cigarettes are placed on the altar for their use. In addition to showing respect to the dead, the family members also greet their deceased ancestors, report recent important family events, and even ask for their wishes, advice, or guidance when making important family decisions. In every way, the family members who have dies are still considered to be present and deeply involved with what the family is doing.

This is especially evident in one of the most important Japanese holidays, the *O-bon* summer festival for the dead. At this time, all the living family members gather together in their ancestral home and invite their dead relatives to come and visit. The visiting spirits are welcomed home, offered food, entertained with dancing and celebrations, and then bid a fond farewell as they return to the realm of the dead. In this way, the continuation of the generations, both past and present, is shared and reaffirmed. All of which makes it perfectly acceptable for a dead loved one to appear to report his recent death, or give comfort in times of trouble.

This is also such a common occurrence in every part of the world that western science has attempted to explain it. Oliver Sacks refers to something he calls "bereavement hallucinations" or "grief hallucinations". He reports in his book, Hallucinations of one study, in which the Welsh doctor, W. D. Rees, interviewed 300 people who had recently lost their spouse, and discovered that almost half of them claimed to have had a visitation from their deceased loved one. He reports that the experience could be "visual, auditory, or both," and that "Some of the people interviewed enjoyed conversations with their hallucinated spouses." (Sacks, 234). He sees these "hallucinations" to be a positive part of the healing process, but never once does it occur to him that something that happens so often with such consistency might be an actual occurrence involving a desired meeting between two loving souls. But these studies involved encounters that happened some time after the spouse had already been informed of the death of the loved one.

There has been no psychological or scientific theory, however, which can explain how a recently dead loved one can appear to someone and announce his death *before* that person has gained any knowledge of that death by any conventional means. Such things make perfect sense in the traditional Japanese concept of family and spirituality. For them, the following stories are an affirmation of the strength of the family bond between the dead and the living.

Grandma in the Kitchen

When I was a child, my family and I lived in a very old house, which my grandfather had built on his own. It was so old that we sometimes saw cockroaches in the kitchen. In the kitchen I used to wash the dishes together with my grandma. But one day my grandmother suddenly felt very weak and she died. We were very sad. I can remember the funeral because, even though I was very young, it was my first experience where any of my relatives had died.

Time passed. One day I was washing dishes in the kitchen. It was a very hot and stuffy day. Then I felt something behind me. I thought it was my mother, so I looked back. There was no one there except this white shadow. It passed by me and disappeared. But strangely, I didn't feel scared.

Thinking back, I am sure that white shadow was my grandmother. And my grandmother had come back to wash the dishes with me! It was nice of you to do so, grandmother! -- Naotaka Tomita

---

Who Was That Girl?

This is a story that my brother experienced. One day, my brother was walking around the house looking for me.

"Yurika, where are you?" he called out.

He opened the door of the Japanese style room where we keep the butsudan (Buddhist altar to the family ancestors), and he found s girl sitting in front of the altar. He thought the girl was I.

"What do you want?" He heard my voice coming from behind him. He quickly turned around to find me standing there.

"What?" he said. Weren't you just sitting over there? "He turned towards the altar again, but there was no one there.

We ran in a hurry to find our mom. "Mom! Mom!"

My brother explained his experience to my mother. Then she told us something we had not known before. Before I was born, my mother had been pregnant with a little girl baby, but, unfortunately, the baby was still born. We think that girl sitting in front of the altar was our sister who wanted to meet us. -- Yurika Matsuoka

A Relative Says Good Bye

I will write about what my mother experienced. It was a quiet night. As usual, she was sleeping, but suddenly she woke up and was held down by a kanashibari. She could not speak or move. The light came on by her bedside.

There was a man standing there who was her relative. He had always been very tender to her when she was a child and she liked him very much.

She tried to say, "What are you doing here?" but she could say nothing. He smiled at her and gradually faded away. Then she could move. The next day she heard that one of her relatives had died. It was the man she had seen the previous day. – Honoka Ohta

Missed Message

This is my mother's story. One night, she dreamed of her uncle. In her dream, he was wearing burial clothes, and he was trying to tell her something, but she woke up before she could catch what he was saying. A few days later her uncle died.

My mother said, "I think uncle wanted to tell me something or wanted me to do something. I had a sense of foreboding when I saw him, but I was not able to meet him long enough to get his message. It makes me sad." -- Saki Shimura

The Sound of Sweeping

I heard this story from my father. My father and mother went to visit my mother's family. This was before I was born. It was during the Obon holiday period. In Japan, it is said that our ancestors come back home during the Obon holiday time. So we burn candles and other lights to signal our ancestors so they can find their way home to visit us.

One night, during this time, my father heard the sound of someone sweeping outside the front door. He thought it was strange because it was late at night, so he wondered who would be out there sweeping in front of the house at this late time.

Later, he told my mother what he had heard. My mother was surprised. She told him that her father who had died a short while before always liked to stand outside and sweep in front of the house as he talked to neighbors and watched what was going on. She was sure it was her father who had come back to visit. -- Yuko Matsunaga

Who Were They?

My mother told me this story. My grandfather was in the hospital with cancer. My mother went to visit him on a day when it was raining very hard. That night she stayed in grandfather's room in the hospital. She went to sleep beside his bed.

In the middle of the night, she woke up. But her body

couldn't move. She heard voices. She looked toward my grandfather and saw some people she didn't know standing around his bed. They were standing near grandfather and talking together, but she couldn't understand what they were saying. Then they faded away. Shortly after that, grandfather died. Mother wonders, who were those people? Ancestors come to take him away? Who were they? -- Keitaro Kawakami.

Little Boy Romping

I am not a spiritual person, so I will tell you about my mother's experience. When my mother was 13, her father (my grandfather) died in an accident. Her mother (my grandmother) was terribly shocked at his death, and her health began to fail. Finally, she was admitted to the hospital

After a while her mother came home, but she was still not well. A short time later, one night, when the whole house was asleep, my mother heard the sound of a little boy playing. My mother looked over by where her mother was sleeping, and she saw a little boy romping by her mother's bed. Suddenly her mother began to suffer. She was gasping as if she couldn't breathe. My mother tried to get up to save her mother, but she couldn't move. She was held down by a kanashibari. She quickly began to pray. She prayed to the little boy not to take her mother away. After she had been praying for a few minutes, the little boy disappeared, and her mother began breathing normally again.

Since that day, my mother has never seen that little boy

again, and my grandmother is still in good health. My mother told me she thinks that boy was her brother who had died as a baby a few months after he was born. She thinks he was very happy to see his father after a long separation, and came to see his mother and wanted her to come with him too. – Maiya Kuze

---

Grandfather's Sandals

My mother experienced this. When she was an elementary school student, her grandfather died. Her grandfather's funeral was held at his house, and she went there with her mother and father. It was a summer day, but a little cool. That night she slept in a large room together with her family.

When the night deepened, she woke up and wanted to go to the bathroom. She was scared to go alone, but all her family were sleeping, so she finally decided to go by herself. As she returned from the bathroom, she heard a noise from the entrance of the house. She wondered if someone was coming in or going out, but she thought it was strange because it was after midnight. She looked at the entrance, but no one was there. Then she heard the sound again. It was the sound of her grandfather's sandals! She ha heard his shuffling step many times and she recognized it immediately.

She went back to bed in a hurry. She was really scared. But when the morning came, she thought it was nice that grandfather had come to say goodbye. -- Miyako Hibino

Vivid Touch

This occurrence happened about one and a half years ago. This is not a scary story, but I want to tell it to you because it is my precious experience. It happened in my house.

At that time, I had been studying throughout the night. I went to bed about 5:00 AM I dreamed. In the dream, I met a man. He was my relative I was surprised because he had died about a half a year before. I talked with him and touched his arm. He touched my arm and squeezed it strongly but affectionately. Then I woke up. I knew that this occurrence wasn't only a dream because the mark of his hand where he had touched me was still vividly there on my arm. I knew that he still existed somewhere. I cried very much after that. -- Erika Miyata

Help Grandma!

This is my grandmother's story. My grandmother's mother, or my great grandmother, died many years ago. And my grandmother took care of her tomb, as is the custom in Japan.

One day, a typhoon hit the city where she lived, and the rain was very heavy. The rain lasted all day and all through the night. As she was sleeping, in the middle of the night, my grandmother had a dream. In the dream her mother was in the old house that she had grown up in. The house was filled with floodwater, and the water was rising fast.

Her mother cried, "Help!" My grandmother tried to reach her mother, but the rising waters pushed her back. Again her mother cried, "Help!" She cried out to her daughter again and again. However hard my grandmother tried to approach her, she could not get close enough to save her.

Then she woke up. The next morning the typhoon had gone, so she decided to go to her mother's tomb to clean up the debris that must have been there. She began to clean up around it. When she opened the repository where the ashes are kept, it was filled with water. She cleared it out, and her mother never bothered her in her dreams again. – (Name withheld by request)

Phone Call

This is my friend's story. His mother told him this story, which happened when he was a baby, about three or four years old.

One day, he was playing with a toy with his mother. Then he said he heard the telephone ringing and picked up the receiver and began talking into it. His mother had not heard any ringing from the phone and was sure he was just playing with the telephone.

After talking into the phone for several minutes, he hung up and said, "Mom, that was grandmother. She said to tell you goodbye."

At that moment, the phone rang for real. His mother

answered the phone and she was surprised. It was the unexpected news that his grandma had just died. (Name withheld by request)

Hitodana

It was a strange event for me. When I was around 8 or 9 years old is when it happened. My family and I were visiting my grandmother's house. The house was a bit old, about fifty years old, and traditional Japanese style. Of course it had a household Buddhist altar or butsudan. At night I slept in the room that had the altar to our dead family members, or the butsuma. It was a usual case for me, because whenever I slept at my grandma's house, I slept there. At that age, I was, of course, sometimes scared. It was a very dark, quiet room with a bit of a spiritual feeling, so every time it felt like a haunted room.

That night, at about midnight, is when it happened. For some reason, I woke up. I saw a glowing light in the room. It was strange that I could see round the room because there had been no light on in that room. There was a bright orange ball that glowed even brighter as I looked at it. It was almost orange, but I couldn't say what the color was exactly. It flew around the room like a fairy and soon it flew away. I fell asleep again, and was awakened when I heard the ringing of the phone in the other room. When I got up that morning I was told that my grandfather had died that night.

I think I really saw my grandfather's corpse candle, or hitodama as we call it in Japanese. I know you might not believe me, but including this event, I have seen a hitodama three times in my life. Each time I saw it just before the deaths of my grandfather, my aunt, and my uncle. I don't know what a hitodama is, exactly, but I think it was a last greeting to me from them. -- Yuki Nomura

Standing by the Gate

My grandmother who lived in Aichi told me this story. One morning my grandmother saw her relative. Her relative was standing outside by the gate to the house.

"Why did she come here?" grandmother asked herself, because her relative lived far away in Yamagata. Then, as grandmother watched, her relative vanished from sight. That night grandmother got a phone call from her relatives living in Yamagata. She was told that that relative had died the morning before. -- Nanae Arao

An Old Man's Voice

This was my sister's experience. When she was 8 years old, she was sleeping in her room alone. She heard an old man's voice. She got up and found an old man standing by her bed. He smiled at her. Then she went to sleep again.

The next day she was told it was the anniversary of her grandfather's death. While her family prayed the traditional prayers for his soul, she looked at his photo. The face was the same as the old man's she had seen the night before. --Nami Sasaki

White Thing

My friend told me this true scary story. About ten years ago, she didn't know why, but she woke up in the night. Without really intending to, she looked out of the window. Then she saw a white thing like a bird floating above her neighbor's house. Then it rose up slowly into the sky until it disappeared. The next day she was told that her neighbor had died suddenly. Was that white thing the old man's soul? – (Name withheld by request)

Hide and Seek

This story is about my terrifying dream. When I was an elementary school student, I dreamed one night of an old woman dressed in white. She appeared in front of me. We had fun playing hide and seek and many other games together. I enjoyed them very much. She told me "thank you", and then she disappeared.

The next day, when I told my sister about it, she said she had had the same dream. I was surprised. Later that day, we learned that our grandma had just died. My sister and I think the old woman we saw in our dream was our grandmother come to say goodbye. – Ayaka Minoura

A Voice in the Library

One day, when I was an elementary school student, I decided to go to the library. Before I went, my sister told me she would also go there later.

"Okay", I said, "I'll see you there later".

At the library, I was reading an interesting book. After a period of time, I heard a whisper.

"Ayana! Ayana!"

I guessed it was my sister calling me, but that book was very interesting. So I decided to ignore the voice. I heard the voice call me two or three times more.

"Ayana! Ayana!"

After a while the voice became softer and then I couldn't hear it any more. I happened to look at the clock about then, and it was 1:30 PM.

That evening, I went back home and asked my sister, "I heard you call me many times. What did you want?"

But my sister replied, "I didn't go to the library today". I was surprised and confused.

Just at that moment, the telephone rang. We answered the phone. It was a call from our grandmother. She said, "Today your great grandmother died peacefully as if she were falling asleep".

We were greatly shocked. Furthermore, she said, "She died about 1:30 this afternoon".

I think it was great grandmother's voice I heard calling my name. Even now, I wonder, if I had answered that voice, what would I have seen? – Ayan Hata

Fathers' Cough

One day I awoke late at night because my father was coughing. It was a very bad cough: it sounded very bad. I became aware of my grandfather standing near my father's bed. At that time, I was too scared to move, because my grandfather had passed away just before that. As my grandfather stood near his bed, my father gradually stopped coughing until he was resting again peacefully. My grandfather disappeared. I believe my grandfather healed or somehow saved my father that night. -- Rika Ohashi

Great Grandfather

When I was a junior high school student, my grandmother was living with her parents-in-law, or my great grand parents. One day my great grandfather died. He was ninety-nine years old. His wife, my great grandmother, couldn't recover from his death. My grandmother worried about her very much.

About a month later, my grandmother woke up at midnight. She looked around and saw my great grandfather was there. My grandmother couldn't believe it because he was clear. She could see through him: he was a ghost! He was wearing a beautiful kimono and he was sitting in seiza (a style of sitting with your legs tucked under you used at formal occasions).

"What are you doing here?" my grandmother asked him.

He said, "I have a lot to thank you for. Please tell Michi I came. Tell her I said hello. "And he vanished. Michi was my great grandmother's name.

My grandmother told what had happened to my great grandmother. At first she cried very much, but when she realized her husband was still somewhere thinking about her, she became fine. -- Rina Miyasaki

Who Is It?

My friend told this story to me. It was a hot night. My friend and his family were sound asleep. Then, the phone rang. At first his mother didn't answer it because she thought it was probably a prank call, but the phone didn't stop ringing. So she answered the phone.

"Sorry to keep you waiting. Who is this?" she said.

But there was no answer. She repeated again. "Sorry. Who is this?" But there as still no answer. She thought it was just a prank call and went back to bed. After two hours, the phone rang again. This time my friend's mother answered the phone in an angry voice, "Who IS this?" she asked.

It was her sister. "This is Yuko. Our mother died two hours ago. Please come to the hospital soon," she said.

Later my friend's mother learned that her sister had gotten a strange phone call at the same time as she had, with no one answering on the other end. They think the call was from their mother. She wanted them to know about her death. This story is a little scary, but a little happy, too. -- Marie Mizuno

A Sutra for Sister

Before I was born, my sister died. About five years ago, at midnight on the anniversary day if her death, the phone rang. My family picked up the receiver. The line was dead. After that, the phone rang again. Again we picked up the receiver, but the line was dead. This was repeated again several times throughout the night. The next day, my family read a sutra for my sister's soul. -- Noburo Inoue

Car Lights

When I was an elementary school student, my teacher told me this story. She was a very spiritual person. One rainy night, she was studying in her room. Suddenly a glaring light shining into her window blinded her. She saw that the bright lights were the headlights of a car, and she was very scared because her room was on the second floor, and there was no possible way a car could be running outside her window. At the very same time, her uncle was killed in a traffic accident while driving on his way home. The car lights she saw must have been from the car her uncle drove as he died. -- Takashi Watanabe

Uncle Knocking

This story is my mother's experience. One day, when

she was an elementary school student, she was sitting in the dining room eating chestnuts with her family. And then, suddenly there was a very loud knocking at the front door. Everyone in the dining room was surprised because the knocking was so loud. Her older brother went to the door to see what was happening. However, no one was there. Ten minutes after that, the telephone rang. Her mother answered the phone. It was from her mother's sister (my friend's mother's aunt).

"Our brother died just now." she said.

Everyone was scared to hear that. They were sure the strange noise at the door was her uncle's soul. He wanted to tell about his death to his relatives. -- Mariko Nakushima

Mother's Dream

This is my mother's real story. One day my grandmother (my mother's mother) fell down because of a brain infarction. She was taken immediately to the hospital, but after a while she died.

A couple of years later, my grandfather (my mother's father) got terribly sick. He had to stay in the hospital for a few weeks, and my mother took care of him all the time in the hospital.

One night, my mother had a dream. She saw my grandmother standing by her bed. She was saying something to my mother, but after she woke up, she couldn't remember what my grandmother had said. That *morning, mother found out that my grandfather had died. Actually the doctor told her he had probably passed away that night about the time she had her dream.*

My mother believes the dream was to tell her that my grandfather would die soon. And my grandmother came to her in the dream tell her she would welcome him, and take him with her. -- Chiaki Sakagawa

Standing At the Door

When I lived in Chiba, There were a lot of houses in the neighborhood that had friends my age. One of my friend's house was about 100 meters from our front door. One evening four years ago, in December, my mother came home from her office at about 6:00 PM. It was getting dark and becoming cold. She saw a man standing in front of my friend's house. Just standing there and not moving at all. As soon as she opened the door and went in, she remembered that she should have gone to the supermarket. She soon went out again. Thirty minutes later, she came back home again. Strangely, the man was still standing in front of my friend's house, still just standing without moving at all.

The next day, my mother called my friend's mother, told her what she had seen, and asked who the man was. My friend's mother's voice sounded like it was shaking, and she said, "My father committed suicide yesterday at about 6:00!" Her father lived far from our town. Did he come there to tell her of his death? She thought maybe it was his ghost. – Takumi Ishizuka

174

The Touch of a Hand

I remember it was a cold day and the sky was clouding over. I was watching TV in my house. Suddenly someone rushed into my house. It was my father. He told me my grandmother was seriously ill and told me to go to the hospital. I was confused with what was happening, but felt there was no time to lose. I got into his car in a hurry without changing my clothes. When I arrived at the hospital and reached the room, I saw that my grandmother was dying. My mother was giving her mother a heart massage with tears in her eyes. I kept calm and took the right hand of my grandmother in my right hand in a strong grip. As I held her hand, she passed away.

Later when I got home, I fell asleep right away. I woke up at four AM and found that I could not move my body at all, but I felt relaxed rather than scared. Then suddenly I felt someone take my right hand. The hand holding mine was warm and I could feel a sense of kindness. I felt as if the touch of that hand was kindness itself. After a while, I was able to move and the hand was gone. I don't know for sure who touched my hand, but I decided it was thanks for when I had taken the hand of my dying grandmother so that she could die peacefully. – -Daisuke Tanaka

Yumi's Story

During one summer vacation, when I was a third year student in elementary school, I saw a ghost. The night I saw him was really muggy, so I slept in my grandmother's room. My grandma and my grandpa used to sleep in the same room. My grandpa would use his big bed and my grandma would sleep on a Japanese style futon-style mattress. Their room was on the first floor and it was Japanese style so it was a little cooler even in summer. I was using his big old bed to sleep in because he had passed away when I was little, and my grandma was sleeping on the Japanese style mattress next to me.

I don't know why but suddenly I woke up and then I looked at the clock to know what time it was. The clock was the type that glowed in the darkness so I could check it. But I realized that there was something strange. I was looking at the clock through something like a haze (it was white but transparent). I looked up, and there was a tall old man standing and staring at me. He had white hair and his face was expressionless and pale. I thought he was angry because of the look on his face. I am 21 years old now but I still remember it clearly. I cannot forget his face. As I looked at his face, I realized he was not a human: he was a ghost. I was so scared. I closed my eyes really tight and hid under the sheet. Maybe after three minutes I quietly showed my face from the sheet to check if he had gone away. He was not there.

Next morning I told my grandma that I had seen a ghost who was a tall old guy with an angry face. My grandma said to me" You were lucky. He must be your grandpa. This season is Obon, so everyone who passed away comes back home, and you saw him."

My grandpa died when I was really small and I only remember that he was lying on the bed in a hospital. I went to the Butsudan and looked at his picture. The face I saw at night was similar to my grandpa. I don't know *what his smiling face looked like, and I don't even know if he ever smiled or not. His face in the picture was very severe. Since then I have not seen any ghost. But I still think of my grandpa and about what he maybe wanted to say to me on that night because he was staring at me. –* Yumi Nishijima

The Tragedy at Tsu City

This story is atypical in that the event was witnessed by many people and was widely reported in the newspapers across Japan after it occurred. The story was told to me by Keiko Tsujioka who was one of the schoolgirls who were present at the time, an eyewitness who lost many of her friends in the disaster. Tsu is a port city in Mie Prefecture and it has a pleasant spot named Kuwahara Beach where the public used to swim. During World War II the charred bodies of many people killed by the bombings were dumped into the water there because there were too many to dispose of properly. Since that time there have been many claims by local people that they have seen the ghosts of the dead stalking the beach at night time.

On July 27th, 1955, the local girls' junior high class was engaged in swimming practice there as they often did since their school had no swimming pool. They swam at this spot because it was always safe, the water was shallow for a good distance from the shore, and they were swimming about fifty meters from the shore where even the shortest of them could stand up and touch the bottom if they got in trouble. It was a bright sunny day, the waves were calm, and everyone seemed to be having a good time.

However on this day, for some reason, several of the girls refused to go into the water and remained watching on the shoreline. Suddenly a wave seemed to rise up. One of the students cried out and disappeared under the water. Then all of the girls began screaming and flailing at the water. They began going under one after the other. Those who could scrambled ashore, and some were saved by nearby fishermen who went out in their boats to rescue them. Thirty-six girls in all drowned that day. Those who survived swore they had felt "big hands" reaching up from the bottom and clutching at them, trying to pull them under. One girl said, "There was a girl wearing a hood like they used to wear for air defense during the war next to me and I nearly drowned because suddenly she pulled my legs".

The incident was widely reported in the Japanese media at the time and it was a major tragedy for the town of Tsu City. Now a statue stands at the site to commemorate the children who drowned there and hopefully to placate the angry ghosts. It is in the shape of a young schoolgirl with angel wings. Swimming is still prohibited at this beach to this day.

Haunted Places

Throughout the history of human kind, there have always been places that were thought to be haunted; places where a supernatural presence seemed to attach itself, and where this presence could be encountered if one were to have the courage go there. In Japan, as in many other countries, these sites are often places associated with death, such as battlefields, hospitals, graveyards, funeral homes, and places where tragedies have occurred. In the past, it was often the custom in Japan to build institutions that were thought to promote good will and compassion, such as temples, schools and hospitals, over the sites of places where, in the past, terrible things had taken place, such as torture sites, graveyards and execution grounds. It was thought that the good will and compassion emanating from the activity in the new positive sites would give peace and comfort to the angry souls who had been formerly caused to suffer there. It was hoped they would be quieted and given rest by being surrounded by the kindness that human beings can show to one another.

But it doesn't always work out that way. Many of the suffering souls don't seem to want to let go of their anger and they still hang around the spots where they met their unfortunate ends expressing their displeasure at the way it happened. As a result, many of the most well known haunted places in Japan seem to be at schools, hospitals and temples.

In every country, horror tales and ghost stories are very popular among the young. And as in other cultures, young people love to test themselves, to do things that can be deemed to be reckless in order to experience a thrill and to test their bravery against each other. Japan is no exception. In Japan, teenagers and young adults have the tradition of *kimodameshi*, or "a test of a person's courage." Haunted places are often used as *kimodameshi* spots where they go, often at night, and challenge each other to see who is the bravest and most foolhardy.

One student wrote an essay in which wrote the rules on how to tell if an apartment or room is really haunted:

These are the ways to distinguish a dangerous room:

1. The cheapest room is always suspicious.

2. Stairs with thirteen steps are dangerous. The room closest to the thirteenth step is the most dangerous.

3. If you suspect a room of being haunted, leave an open cup of sake out in the middle of the room. Leave for a short while. If, when you come back, the sake has soured, the room is dangerous.

Dangerous River

This is a story from my hometown. I heard this story from my grandmother. There is a big river that runs through my town. When it rains for a long time, the river becomes full, and it sometimes causes a big flood. Because of this, a lot of people were drowned to death in the old days. It is said that the river is dangerous. The ghosts of the people who died in the flood are often seen there.

It happened on a day when my grandmother was ten years old. It was a very hot day. In the morning, she and her friends were playing with a ball. They had splashed mud on their dresses, so they went to the river to wash the mud off of their dresses. One of her friends was afraid. She said that they should not go there because the ghosts of the people who had died were there. Another girl said there was no such thing as ghosts in the world, so they went to the river.

By the time they got to the river, it was afternoon. They started to wash off their dresses, but it was a hot day, so they started swimming in the river. My grandmother was swimming in the river when suddenly she felt someone grab her leg. It grabbed her and was trying to pull her down beneath the water. She struggled against it, but it was very strong: she almost drowned. Finally she kicked hard, and got free, and got out of the river.

After she got out of the river, she asked her friends who had grabbed her leg, but her friends were all there at the side of the river. There was no one who could have grabbed her leg. When she got home, she looked at her leg. There was a bruise in the shape of a human hand on her leg. – (Name withheld by request).

A Boy in Pajamas

My mother is s nurse and she used to work in Ama Central Hospital in Amagun, Aichi Prefecture. This hospital was a general hospital and the biggest in the area.

One evening, she was the night nurse, and she was walking the dark hallways with a flashlight. Then she found a little boy wearing pajamas and pulling along an intravenous drip standing there in the hallway. She asked him if he needed to go to the bathroom. He didn't answer; he just turned and went up stairs. She wondered what he was doing, and she followed him shouting, "Stop!"

Finally she reached the top floor, and there was no little boy. There was nobody there, just the locked door to the rooftop. When she told her co-workers about what she had seen, several of them said that they had also seen the ghost of the little boy several times before. (Name withheld by request)

Bad Feng Shui

There are some ruins called sankaku-yashiki in my hometown of Jimokuji. It's an abandoned house that has some rumors about psychic phenomena. The rumors of this house began to spread about 30 years ago. At that time, a young couple bought the land and built the house, but the husband soon committed suicide. Since then, although several different tenants have lived there, they all left soon because their families all met with misfortunes, such as suicides or fatal accidents. At present there are many rumors about the house and there is no telling what is the truth. It is true, however that the land the house is built on is in the shape of a triangle. The lay of the land in this shape gives the worst effect on the house and the fate of the people living in it according to the art of Feng Shui. Some people go there to do kimodameshi, and sometimes they become scared when they meet the ghosts of the people who died there. – Yuji Okamura (Note: kimodameshi is the act of going to a frightening place to challenge each other and prove your bravery).

Girl Ghost

When I was in elementary school, there was a quiet girl in my class. She was never a cheerful girl, so the other students in the fifth grade bullied her. Later, the girl was killed. The criminal was her own father. He went crazy and killed the mother, brother, and her. Then he killed himself in a family murder-suicide. After that, there were rumors of many people seeing the ghost of that girl walking in the yard around her home. I don't know if the rumors were true or not, but still now, so many years later, no one lives there. The house is covered with blue vinyl sheets. (Name withheld by request)

Schoolgirl

I heard this story from my high school teacher and my friend who was a student there. It happened during the summer when we were in twelfth grade.

It was after dark. My teacher was walking down the hallway, passed one classroom, and saw a little girl inside the room. She was wearing a school uniform and crouching down with her back to the door. My teacher thought it was strange because such a young student was not supposed to be in that room, and was not supposed to be in the school so late.

Later, my friend was going down the hallway to see our teacher and she also saw the little girl in the room, but couldn't see her face. When she told the teacher about seeing the girl, they both returned immediately to the room, but there was no girl inside, and the door was locked. There was no way anyone could have gotten in that room.

After that, two of my friends, who have the inspiration to see ghosts (riekan ga suyoi), said they felt a cold chill whenever they passed that room. Clearly there was something strange in that room. -- Yuika Hamada

Ghost Highway

This is a story, which my friend from my junior high school days told me. When he became a college student, he was looking for an apartment to rent, and he soon found a nice tidy place that he liked. Also, the rent was very low, so he decided to live there.

After he was there for several days, he found some strange thing kept happening. When he went to bed each night, he found that each night, he would be attacked by a kanashibari and he would be unable to move his hands or feet. When he went to bed he would also hear strange sounds. It would sound like someone was rushing up the stairs outside at a terrible speed right to his door. It was very loud, but every time he looked, there was no one there.

He got scared, so he placed piles of salt in each corner of the room to purify it. When he came home, he would find the salt scattered around the room, even though he had locked the door and the windows before he left.

He couldn't stand the situation, so he talked to a friend who was sensitive to the spirit world. He and she decided to go to the apartment. As they were walking toward his apartment, she suddenly stopped, pointed ahead, and said, "Is that your apartment?"

He was very surprised because he hadn't told her which building or room was his, but she had guessed it immediately.

She said, "That place is in the middle of a ghost road. That is a place where many spirits pass through. So I recommend that you move out of that apartment."

Following her advice, he moved into another apartment, and he had a peaceful life there. -- Yuri Ibuki

Restaurant

In my town, Mizuho Undojo, there is a popular spaghetti restaurant. The name of the restaurant is Hiroshi. That was the owner's name. But the owner died a few years ago.

After he died, all of the workers at the restaurant began experiencing psychic phenomena; for example, they heard the sound of someone eating spaghetti, although there was no one in the restaurant at the time and some saw the shadow of a man moving in the room, but there was nobody there. The wife of the owner said, "It's Hiroshi. He's checking on the workers here."
To tell the truth, I'm working at that restaurant, and I've heard the eerie sound many times. The story is true. -- Megumi Oka

Not a Customer

This is my friend's story. There is a Japanese crab restaurant and she works there as a part-timer. After she had worked there for a while, she heard many strange stories about the restaurant. The stories are about two ghosts that are there.

One day, one of the employees she knew saw a man entering the kitchen. He had never seen the man before, so he assumed he was a customer. He wondered, "What is he doing going into the kitchen?" So he told the owner about it.

"Oh, he's not a customer", the owner said. "He's a ghost. We see him all the time." The owner didn't look scared at all. "He's often here walking around," he said.

The other story is about a woman wearing a kimono. Some employees talked about seeing her in the restaurant. My friend saw her, too. One night when she had finished her job, she, the owner, and another employee came out of the restaurant. It was 2:00 AM. Of course, they had turned off all the lights in the restaurant. However, she saw a red light shining through the window. She thought, "Did I forget to turn off a light?"

But she was wrong. She looked in the window and saw a woman wearing a kimono standing near the red light. My friend was very surprised, and told the other two.

"Really?" the owner said, and they all looked in the window. However, this time, there was no light and no woman. -- Rika Egi

Ghost on the Bridge

This is a scary story from my boyfriend. Seven years ago, when he was a university student, he was driving his car alone at night. It was summer, and there was a heavy rain at midnight. Because of the bad weather, he could *not see the road very well.*

On the way to go back home from Gifu to Aichi, he drove across the Aikyou Bridge, which is the connecting bridge between Gifu and Aichi. There were few cars on the road, so he turned right at the intersection without slowing down. Then, he saw an old woman with white hair and wearing a purple kimono step into the road in front of him. He put on the brakes, but it was too late. He ran right over the woman.

He jumped out of the car with a lot of fear, bur when he looked, there was no one there. Suddenly, he got very scared when he thought about the moment he had hit her. He had not felt anything when his car touched her because there was no sound of him hitting something. As soon as he realized this, he got a kind of horror feeling. He got back in his car and drove away very fast.

A few years later, he told this story to his friend who lived in Gifu. His friend said he had had a similar experience in that spot. According to his friend, a long time ago, there was a flood in the river that ran under the bridge, and a lot of people died. Since that tragedy happened, many people driving their cars on that bridge have seen the ghosts of the people who died in the flood. – - Yuko Watanabe

Supermarket

At the local supermarket near my home, there used to be many mysterious phenomena happening. The display cases would fall down suddenly, and the doors would

close, even thought here was no one around and no wind. Such strange things continued without cessation, so the workers in the supermarket, and the customers all began to have a horrible feeling about that place. As a result, the supermarket had fewer customers, and fewer people who would work there. It soon began to face business difficulties.

The truth is that they found out the supermarket was in a building that was used as a temporary morgue when there were too many bodies during the war. It was said that the souls of those who had died there might have been unable to rest in peace. The owners of the supermarket decided to have it purified by a priest. After that the mysterious phenomena stopped. They still have it purified once a year, every year. -- Aya Mukai

Jizo

My grandmother told me this story:

"When I was a junior high school student, there was a ma-no-yotsutsuji (an intersection where many accidents happened) near my home. Every year, somebody died there. One day, a truck hit a little boy (I will call him 'A' in this story), and it crashed into the garden of our house. The little boy died. So A's mother decided to place a Jizo, a statue of a deity that is the guardian of little children, in our garden. Surprisingly, no accidents occurred for a long while after that.

However, it was so close to the road that, each time a truck ran past, the Jizo shook a lot, and eventually it

cracked and its head fell off. It looked very inauspicious, so A's mother decided to take the Jizo and put it in a temple. Before long, A's mother died in a car accident right at the ma-no-yatsuji intersection!

Why were there so many accidents at that intersection? Why did no traffic accident occur while the Jizo was standing there? Why did A's mother have to die? I don't know, but I hope there are no accidents there now. We moved away from there in 1979, and I don't know about it since then."

"I know," I said to my grandmother, "the Jizo protected the people from disasters, right?"

"Maybe," she said. -- Mina Suzuki

Priest

It was a damp evening during rainy season. My friend and I were walking at Atsuta Shrine in the evening when suddenly we both stopped. We couldn't move, we were frozen to the spot.

"I can't move," I said to my friend.

I didn't know what was happening. I felt a very scary mood. Suddenly I saw a man walking toward us. He was dressed like a Shinto priest. He was dressed all in white.

He approached us very slowly, but we still couldn't move. My mind went blank as I watched him. He walked toward us, but he never came near us. We watched as he *disappeared starting with his legs and then up to his head. I thought it was an illusion, but my friend saw the same thing. Even now I am still scared of that spot. I will never walk in Atsuta Shrine at night again!* -- Masahiro Suzuki

Subway Ghost

Do you usually use the Higashiyama subway line? I think everyone in Nagoya uses it. The Higashiyama line runs from Fujigaoka station to Takabata, by way of Nagoya station.

Have you ever felt that there were many stations between Fujigaoka station to Fushimi, but between Fushimi and Nagoya, there is a long way without a station? In fact, Nagoya City was originally going to make another station between Fushimi and Nagoya, but it was called off when a man was buried alive in a cave-in when the station was under construction.

And, yes, the ghost of the dead man is still there. At night, when you get on the last rain from Fujigaoka station to Nagoya station, if you watch carefully out the front window of the first car, you will see his ghost outside on the tracks. Many people have seen him. -- Yu Takashima

Kimono Service Girl

It was Monday August 12th, 1985. Many people were planning to go home for summer vacation by airplane. One Japan Airlines plane left Haneda Airport in Tokyo at

6:12 PM bound for Itami Airport in Osaka. Who would have guessed then that the airplane would have a terrible accident?

Because it was the beginning of summer vacation, the plane was very crowded. The female cabin crewmembers were doing "Kimono Service" in which they wore traditional kimonos and served Japanese-style snacks. All the people on the plane seemed to be enjoying themselves, and were looking forward to landing in Osaka soon, but the plane crashed in Gunma Prefecture only 44 minutes after taking off.

There were 524 people on the plane, but only four people survived. 520 people died in that crash! And the strange thing was that all the survivors were women. One of them was a cabin crewmember that was 26 years old. Two others were a 34-year-old mother and her 8-year-old daughter. The other was a 12-year-old girl. That's all. Only four women survived!

After the horrible accident, Japan Airlines decided not to do the Kimono Service any more, as it was decided that the Kimono Service was one of the biggest reasons why all but one of the cabin crew didn't get out of the plane. When women wear kimonos, they cannot move easily, and it is difficult for them to run fast. In the airplane crash, the female crewmembers could not move fast enough to save themselves.

Later, at Itami Airport, some of the crew who clean out the airplanes were startled to saw a woman wearing a kimono on the airplane. One of the cleaners said she saw the figure of a woman that was all white. She seemed to *be going about her duties as a cabin crewmember before she disappeared. The woman was seen many times on airplanes that should have only had the cleaning crew on board.*

People say she is the ghost of one of the cabin crew who was doing Kimono Service on the plane that crashed on August 12th 1985. Her body could not land at Itami Airport, but her spirit and her heart really wanted to land there safely with all the cabin crew and customers. Her spirit and her heart are still there and she is busy happily doing her job and serving the people. – Mina Kobayashi

Clock for Peace

In my city, there was a street that was well known for having many traffic accidents happen there. The visibility there was not bad, but, still, many people had accidents on that street. Even the police couldn't explain why that street had so many accidents. Whenever someone died, the people would leave flowers by the road for him or her.

One day, a girl named Rika passed by on that street in the early morning. She was a junior high school student, and it was her first day to go to junior high school. She was riding a new bicycle, and had just crossed the street when a car hit her. Sadly, she died in the accident. Many people grieved for her.

To stop any further accidents, her mother had a clock built where her daughter had died. Her mother named the clock with her daughter's nickname, "Ri-chan's

193

clock". On the clock, written in large letters, were the words, "Take five minutes longer and drive safely".

After the clock was built, the number of accidents decreased sharply. And people say that, if you look at just the right time, you can see Ri-chan standing by the clock, keeping her eyes on the street, and hoping for peace for everybody. – Kyoko Sugiyura

Jizo Apartment

There is an apartment building near our house. All around the site, there are many Jizo statues. Jizos are usually found in temples, and it is very strange to see them in front of an apartment building. So I asked my parents about it. They told me this story:

From the time the apartment was built, there were many bad happenings, and all of these bad happenings concerned children. Children who lived there were often injured. Some got terribly sick, and some died. People found out that, in the past, there had been a hospital in that place, and it was thought that there was something evil left there from all the people who had died there. Perhaps this was having a bad effect on the children.

So the people who lived there decided to put up the statues of Jizo, who is the patron god who protects children. They put up the Jizos and prayed, and, strangely enough, the bad things stopped happening. But the Jizos remain there today, protecting the children and keeping them safe.-- Maiko Higashiyama

They Forgot

A few years ago, there was a plan to build an apartment building in our neighborhood. In Japan, we usually have a priest hold a purification ceremony before the beginning of the construction in order to provide protection from bad influences. But at that time, they started to build without doing the purification ceremony. After the apartment was completed, there were several suicide leaps from the roof, and many traffic accidents in the road right in front of the building. So the people called in a priest and held a purification ceremony. Since then, there have bee no accidents or strange deaths there. -- Ayaka Kawai

(Note: The following is part of an article I originally wrote for *Avenues* Magazine when I was a reporter and editor there).

Ghost Hotel

A couple of years ago, work began on the New Tokoname Kanko Hotel. There were many problems that occurred during its construction and the construction crew developed especially uneasy feelings about the project they were working on. For one thing, there were several times the workers refused to leave the work site at the end of the day because some of the men swore they could see an old man and woman sitting in the courtyard who had no faces. Others said they couldn't see them at all.

When the hotel was opened, it had a Chinese restaurant

on the fifth floor. Chisato Yoshigawa, formerly one of the workers there, reports that often, when the staff arrived at eight o'clock in the morning to prepare the food for the day, they saw the misty outlines of three men sitting in the restaurant. The figures would be fairly distinct at first, and then would slowly fade away as the astounded restaurant workers watched. The figures were always sitting in the same seats, and they were seen so often that the staff soon developed the habit of greeting each other, not with *"Good morning!"* but with, *"Today they were here",* or, conversely, *"They weren't here today."*

Later, a rumor surfaced that there was once a factory on the site in which three men were killed in an industrial accident. Today, only a few years after it was opened, the hotel stands closed and deserted, and a tall fence has been erected around the site to keep the curious away. This reporter was unable to find anyone who could explain why.

Kokkurisan

Japanese girls often play a game that works a lot like the Ouija Board found in America and other Western countries. They write the Japanese *hiragana* alphabet on a piece of paper along with *hai* (yes) and *ie* (no) on a piece of paper. Sometimes the numbers one through ten are added. A five-yen coin, which has a hole in the middle, is placed on the paper, and two girls each place a finger lightly on either side of the coin. They then call up the spirit of *Kokkurisan* (also called *Kokkurisama), who is* the trickster Fox God who figures in many Japanese folk tales, and ask him questions. He replies by moving the coin across the paper and as each letter appears in the round hole of the coin, the answer is spelled out. But there are strict rules on how to go about this. If the rules are not followed to the letter, it can have dangerous results. One friend reported that, when she was in junior high school, she and her friends consulted *Kokkurisan* without dismissing him properly at the end. After that, the room of the school where they had preformed the ritual was haunted by the shadow of a fox that frightened the girls until a priest was called in to exorcise the place. Following are some first hand accounts of those who performed the *Kokurisan* ritual and the subsequent results.

(Note: There are many variations on this ritual in Japan. *Sometimes a ten-yen coin is used instead of a five-yen coin.* In some locations, a similar ritual using a pen, often called "spirit writing" in the West, is referred to as *Bunshinsaba.*)

Kokkurisan Rules

There aren't any children in Japan that don't know about Kokkurisan. It is said that Kokkurisan foretells your fortune and misfortune. If you ask him to curse someone, he will grant it. He can even kill someone who is cursed.

It is a very unique way that we invite Kokkurisan to come to this world, and most Japanese people have done it at least one time.

First, you prepare a paper. Second, you write the hiragana or gojyuon on it. Third, you get a ten-yen coin.

Fourth, you write "yes" or "no" at the top of the paper. Fifth, you put your forefinger on the coin and place it between "yes" and "no". Finally, you ask him something, and then the coin moves to answer of its own accord. Watch out! If you don't throw away the ten-yen coin at the end, he'll curse you! -- Ayaka Kaiden

Kumiko's Real Story

This is a real story. When I was an elementary school student, my classmates and I were lying on the ground one warm night, observing the heavenly bodies above. A lot of cicadas were singling loudly. Then three of my classmates proposed to try Kokkurisan. Kokkurisan is a popular Japanese psychic phenomenon. Kokkurisan is the spirit of a fox. We call on Kokkurisan when we do the ritual. To prepare we need a paper, a pen, and a Japanese coin. So they prepared the tools, and then they started to do Kokkurisan.

I didn't take part because I felt horribly scared about Kokkurisan, so I watched them from afar. They started to do it in the middle of the ground under the night sky. That night, the wind was strong, and kept blowing for some time after they finished.

"How was it doing Kokkurisan?" I asked them.

"We called his name and he talked to us!" they said. They were very excited.

They were so excited they forgot the rules. One rule is that, when you are done, you have to tear up the paper

and burn it. They tore up the paper, but didn't burn it, and the rush of the wind carried the pieces of paper away. And they didn't use the right coin when they did it, either.

The next day, I went to school as usual. But one of the girls who had done Kokkurisan was absent from school with a high fever. The next day, another one of them was absent from school with a high fever. And the day after that, the last one was home with a high fever. I was very scared! – (Name withheld by request)

A Way of Fortunetelling

This was told to everyone when we were elementary school students. Kokkurisan is a way of fortunetelling. You write hiragana characters on a white paper. Also, you write "yes" and "no" at the side of the hiragana characters. At the top in the middle, you draw a picture of a torii, the gate at the entrance to a Shinto shrine that tells it is on sacred ground. Now you are ready to call Kokkurisan.

You gather with more than one person, four is best. You put a ten yen coin in front of the torii, and everybody's forefinger has to be on the coin. Then you say, "Kokkurisan, Kokkurisan, please rise before us!" Then the coin will be moved by Kokkurisan's spirit. Here, it is thought that Kokkurisan possesses you.

Next you ask what you want about your fortune, for example, "Will Mr. Tanaka be able to get the girl Ms. Fujita?" Then the coin would move to "yes" or "no". You can also ask how, where, when and what questions as well, not just yes or no questions.

When you finish fortunetelling, you must announce, "Kokkurisan, Kokkurisan, please leave us now!" If you don't say these last words, everyone who played the game will be cursed. Also, during the augury, everyone should not let go of your forefinger on the coin. If you do, something bad will happen and at the worst, you will die! -- Junko Sasaki

Last Time *Kokkurisan*

When I was an elementary school student, Kokkurisan was very popular. I did it many times. One day, while doing Kokkurisan, with six friends, we couldn't finish properly. It was difficult to finish correctly because Kokkurisan has a lot of rules, for example: (1.) Don't lift your fingers from the coin; and (2.) If you don't want Kokkurisan to follow you back to your home, you have to tear the paper into 100 to 200 pieces when you are finished.

We did everything mostly right: we didn't lift our fingers from the coin. But when we were finished, we were in a hurry and didn't tear the paper into 100 pieces. After a while, we began to feel bad. We had such a bad feeling and became so scared, that we went to a shrine to pray for help. After that, the teacher told us to stop doing Kokkurisan. -- Aya Mintani

Bunshinsaba

(Note: a Korean university student studying in Japan told this story to me. *Bunshinsaba* is a game of divination similar to *Kokkurisan*. When doing *Bunshinsaba*, two people hold a pen between them and call on the spirit of *Bunshinsaba*, the ghost of a young girl. *Bunshinsaba* then comes and moves the pen to point to the figures on the paper and spell out the answers to their questions. Young Koreans and Japanese may have gotten this ritual from a Korean horror movie of the same name that was released in 2004. It was popular in many countries throughout Asia and was also released in the United States.).

When I was in high school, it was popular to play a game called Bunsinhsaba, which is similar to the game Ouija Board.

One day my study partner asked me, "Why don't we play Bunshinsaba?"

"Sorry, I don't want to play", I said. I wasn't interested in playing a game that wasn't real.

"Come on, let's play!" she said. She grabbed my hands, joining them with her hands. She inserted the pen in our hands and began playing. She began to utter the incantation.
At first I could tell she was controlling the movement of the pen. But after a few seconds, the pen began to move by itself. I couldn't believe it! The pen was moving without our control!

I was getting scared. "It's working!" she said. She started asking many questions: "Will I go to the university?" "Will I get married?" etc.

I still didn't want to play. "I'm going to quit now, okay?" I told her. But she didn't want me to quit.

"She says she doesn't want to keep going," she said to the spirit of Bunshinsaba. You still want to play with her, right?" she said, facing the paper.

I didn't want to play any more so I pulled my hands away. Then the pen began moving faster in her hands.

"Come on!" she said. "She will be angry if you don't come back and play!"

I didn't want to play any more, so she gave me a disgusted look and moved to another seat and kept on playing.

That night I couldn't sleep at all. I was scared and felt something terrible was going to happen. I can't explain how bad I felt except to say I've never had an experience like that again and I hope I never do. I didn't see my study partner for a while after that, and I never really wanted to talk to her again. Sometimes I think about that day and wonder what became of my study partner, if she was all right after that. -- Jaehee Lee

Ghost Hotel

(Note: The following story was part of an article I wrote

that first appeared in *Nagoya Avenues Magazine*).

Just outside of Tajimi City in Gifu Prefecture stand the broken remains of an old hotel. It has been abandoned for quite some time, and has been subject to a lot of vandalism, but only the truly brave go there at night. The hotel was erected over a hot spring and it was once very popular with tourists coming to relax for a time with a soak in the hot mineral water and breathe in the fresh country air. The story is that part of the hotel was destroyed in a gas explosion. Several people were killed and the owners abandoned the hotel after the catastrophe occurred. Now the place is haunted: the ghosts of the people who died in the explosion and subsequent fire still stomp around the old hotel, resentful about their tragic and untimely deaths. One tale often told about the place is that a famous psychic once tried to enter the hotel, but was unable to because the malevolent power of the ghosts was too strong. So, one fine Sunday evening, I decided to enter the hotel along with several intrepid friends to see what we could turn up in the way of psychic impressions.

When we first arrived, there was a group of young Japanese teenagers running through the first floor of the hotel shouting *yada!* (I don't like it!), and *kowai!* (I'm scared!). Not a very hopeful beginning for a gothic horror story. After a while, however, the young ones left and we moved deeper into the bowels of the hotel. One of our group, a New Zealander, offered up a Maori prayer of greeting to the dead, and we climbed the stairs to the upper floors of the building.

The place had been repeatedly trashed by many waves of vandals, and one section of it clearly showed that there had once been a very bad fire there. We encountered many huge black spiders complete with creepy hanging webs to put us in the proper mood, but to our disappointment, we could find no gibbering specters scuttling down the hallways, no disembodied voices urging us to jump out of upper floor windows.

We finally emerged onto what once must have been a balcony overlooking a swiftly running river below. We sat down around an old dingy table and looked overhead at the cold star-filled sky, and listened to the gurgling of the rushing river below us. Here a Japanese lady named Kaori took out a piece of paper with Japanese *hiragana* written on it, placed a five-yen coin on the paper, and announced that we should call up the spirit of *Kokkurisama* in order to communicate with the ghosts. Kaori and I each placed a finger on opposite sides of the coin. She then called forth the spirit of *Kokkurisama*, and when he indicated he was present, we began a question and answer session. It's difficult to say why these things work, and it is very possible that one of us was subconsciously manipulating the coin, but I don't think so. Here is the resultant conversation. Our questions are in regular type, and the ghostly answers are in creepy bold type:

Kokkurisama, are there any ghosts here? *Yes!*

How many? *Four!*

Are they happy? *Yes!*

Are they dangerous? *Yes!*

Are they dangerous to us? *Yes!*

What should we do? *Go Home!*

Can we help the ghosts? *Yes!*

How? *Stop what you are doing, NOW!*

And so we did. And we went home. What would you have done?

Personal Experiences

Many people who have a run-in with the supernatural only experience it once. These are the stories of people who have had that one significant meeting with a ghostly presence. While most of them have no clue as to the history or the story behind whatever it was they encountered, it is an encounter that will remain with them for the rest of their lives. In almost every case, it is a moment they will never forget; a moment that redefined for them what is possible and impossible in this world. As they tell their stories, many of them do so with a puzzled expression on their faces. Many of them end their stories with the question of, "*What was that?*"

Teachers Find the Answer

When I was a junior high school student, I heard this story from my cram school teacher. One day, my teacher was teaching a class in an elementary school. One student came in late for class because his school friend had died and he had attended the funeral. After the funeral, he had come to class. In a very short time, students started getting sick. In fact, so many students got sick that the teachers could not teach the class. The teachers met and discussed what to do. They found the answer in traditional Japanese culture. In Japan, after a funeral, we scatter some salt behind us as we leave so the spirit of the recently deceased person can't follow us back home. They asked the boy if he had done this, and he said, "No". The teachers then scattered salt to the four corners of the school, and the class returned to its usual peaceful condition. And the teaching could continue. This is a true story. – -Maika Suzuki

Zashiki-Warashi

A while ago, I worked in a department store in the downtown Sakae area of Nagoya, selling fresh juice to the customers. I met many kinds of people, some of them strange.

I would like to tell you about one elderly woman. She was about 80. However, her appearance was quite peculiar. The department store I worked at had many kinds of customers, but most of them looked elegant and rich. This lady, however, did not apply. She looked miserable and eccentric.

She came to my store and seemed to be shopping for juice. I asked her which juice she would like to buy, but she kept speaking next to her. I thought she had come with company, but when I looked beside her, I soon realized there was no one there but her. I guess she was speaking next to her for about five minutes, which is a long time! Finally, she walked away, still talking to someone who was invisible. Maybe she and her unseen company couldn't come to a conclusion of which juice to buy.

I told this story to my co-worker. She told me that that old woman sometimes came into the store, and she was always talking with someone you couldn't see. Once when my co-worker talked to the woman, she told her that she was always with her friend, who was a "Zashiki-Warashi", which is a Japanese ghost that brings good luck. A Zahiki-Warashi is a ghost that looks like a young child and inhabits your house. If you treat it kindly, it will bring good fortune to you and your household. The lady said her Zashiki-Warashi was with her always, protecting her and bringing her good luck.

A few months later, I saw her again in the store. That time, she also said something to her company, but I could see no one. -- Yuri Mamiya

White Dress

When my father was 26 years old, he was simply lying down on his bed one night. There was no sound, and nothing was moving. He looked up from his bed, and it was so dark, he was blind as a bat. Then he saw it. A white flowing dress on a very faint and very pale woman. He swears he had never seen anything like it before. She flowed with light. She was like a shadow, he couldn't see any physical features, but there was a white flowing dress with light shining out of it. What was that? -- Ryota Asao

Long Life

My mother told me this story. The men who came from my grandfather's family line all died sooner than other people. My grandfather's three brothers all died when they were young. Mysteriously, none of them were able to live for a long time.

My grandfather was very worried about this, so he went

to a temple. The Buddhist priest there heard his story, prayed on the matter, and then said, "A woman who was in your family line died and was not given a proper burial in our family grave. So you should hold a religious service for her." My grandfather researched and found that a while back, such a woman existed. So my grandfather did what the priest said.

Now my grandfather is 78 years old and full of energy. I hope he will live for a long time. – Yui Okaniwa

A Child's Face

My friend's mother told me this. She was cleaning up, pulling weeds around her family's graveyard in the mountains. She happened to raise her eyes, and saw that there was a child looking directly at her from behind a gravestone.

"You shouldn't be playing in a graveyard," she said. But a moment later, when she walked to the gravestone to talk to the child, the child was gone, and she could see that the gravestone was on the edge of a cliff and there was no place there for a child or anyone to stand. She was looking behind the gravestone but the child had vanished as of it had been absorbed into the grave.

"Strangely," she said, "I didn't feel scared, just kind of sad. So I offered a flower to the grave and put my hands together in prayer." – Masumi Yamada

The Closet Door

This is a story I experienced some years ago. One quiet night, I was aware of a change. For no reason, the sliding door to the closet in my room was open. The closet was heavy and filled with many things we did not usually use. At first, I didn't think about it so much, and I just closed it. However, even though no one in my family touched the door, after that it was open every day after that. We closed the door again and again, but it was opened again immediately when we didn't notice. The opening was always narrow, about 15 centimeters, as if someone was looking into the room from inside the closet. My father checked inside of it, of course, but there was nothing in there except the things we were storing in there. In short, it seemed that the door was opening by itself!

We began to think it was strange, and we consulted my grandmother about it. She said, "I am worried that this is connected to your sister and her family".

My father's sister had been killed, along with her husband and child, in a traffic accident. My grandmother had a little bit of inspiration about such things and she felt something was wrong.

In addition, my father had just had a series of car accidents, one after another, and we were worried about him. The accidents and the recent incidents with the opening door were strange, so the family decided to invite a Buddhist priest to the house. My parents explained what was happening, and the priest read a sutra and spoke words of condolences to the dead. After that, the door never opened again, and my father never had another traffic accident again.

I don't know if these things were caused by my aunt's death, and were solved by the Buddhist priest, but I can't forget what happened, and it still seems strange to me. Through this experience, I came see that it is important to be aware of death and to be thankful for living a good and healthy life. -- Hitomi Akabari

The Motorcycle

My mother and her friend went out on a drive in a car late at night in order to go to the top of a near-by mountain and watch shooting stars. They were driving on a very dark road on the mountain, and when they turned a curve, they came to an intersection. The driver stopped because the traffic light was red. The driver noticed a motorcycle in front of the car with a man riding on it. The driver saw it, but my mother did not see it, so she said to the driver, "Why are you stopping so far back? Why don't you move closer to the light?"

"Because of that motorcycle in front of us," the driver said.

"What motorcycle?" asked my mother. The driver looked at her with a puzzled expression on her face.

After a while, the light changed from red to green. "Okay, let' go," said the driver, but the motorcycle in front of them had disappeared without making a sound. "Where is the motorcycle?" she said.

Then both of the women looked to the left of the roadside and saw the kind of small shrine they put up for someone who has been killed recently in a traffic accident. There was a bouquet of fresh flowers and a portrait of the man who had been killed sitting there by the side of the road. --Tatsuya Kondo

The Strange Man

This is my real experience. Maybe some can believe this, but some cannot. At that time, I couldn't believe what happened, because I saw a ghost!

When I was in junior high school, I got heavy sick. I couldn't go to school, and I had to stay in the hospital. My body and my mind became weaker and weaker. One day, my doctor allowed me to go back home for one night, and I was very happy. My parents picked me up at the hospital. Then I went back to my home, and spent a relaxed time with my family.

After that, I went shopping with my mother, and I had a good time. On the way home, we were stopped at a traffic light, waiting for the signal to change to green. Many cars were waiting for the signal to change. As I was looking to the front, I saw someone coming from the right. It was a man. He was crossing the street very slowly. He was wearing a white tee shirt and jeans, and he had round shoulders. He passed in front of our car. Our car's corner sensors rang. I wondered why the man was crossing there. It was a dangerous place in the middle of the street, and what's more, he was moving very slowly. I felt it was very strange.

After he had passed, I said to my mother, "That man was very strange, wasn't he?"

My mother said, "Man? What are you talking about?"

"The man who just passed in front of our car!"

"In front of our car?" My mother didn't understand what I was talking about.
"Yes!" I said. "Didn't you see him?"

"No! No one passed by here. Are you all right?"

"But our car sensors rang when he walked in front of our car! Didn't you hear that?"

"Yes, I heard that, but no one was there!"

Maybe, at that time, I had become weaker because of my illness. Maybe it made me more sensitive to many things. And that's why I could see the ghost. – -Sachi Nagaya

A Woman In the Dark

This is a real story from my older sister's experience. She is a very spiritual person, so that she has seen many ghosts before. Whenever she sees a ghost, she tells me about it, but the weird thing is she is never afraid of them. From the stories she has told me, I think this is the scariest one, which is about a woman in a white wedding dress in the dark.

This happened when she was a high school student. On that day, she was so tired because she had a lot of homework. After she had finished her homework, she went to bed. It was about two o'clock in the morning. When she was sound asleep, a big noise woke her up. It was a strange noise that she had never heard before.

She got up, and walked toward where the noise was coming from. The noise gradually became louder and louder. When she entered the hallway, suddenly, she saw a white object.

It was a tall young woman wearing a white wedding dress. She was walking very slowly down the corridor. She passed by my sister and then she was gone. She disappeared! We still have no idea who that woman was. -
– Kana Hirano

Ghosts and Shamans in Okinawa

Last summer I was hired to teach a special intensive 12-day seminar in English to some company employees of a very large and famous Japanese company. The seminar took place in Okinawa, and I got to know Keiko, the lady who managed the school that had hired me, and her partner, Tachan. They did their best to make me feel at home, and to introduce me to Okinawan culture and history. Although it is a part of Japan today, Okinawa, the southern most group of islands in Japan, was formerly its own kingdom, sometimes referred to as the Ryuku Islands, until it was taken over by Japan. It is, in many ways, still a culture unique from the rest of Japan with its own set of religious practices and belief systems. The Okinawans live in a world that is inhabited by nature spirits, shamans, the ghosts of dead ancestors, and many other occult forces.

When traveling around some of the islands of Okinawa, you will often encounter a statue of *Kijimuna*, a small impish-looking ogre with red hair and a bright purple face. He is said to be a tree spirit that lives in a Gajumaru tree, and he is a naughty trickster spirit who pulls many pranks on people. The statues are put up to appease him so he will leave the local people alone and not bother them. He will sometimes come to you at night when you are sleeping and hold you down so you can't move (another form of *kanashibari*). The only way to get rid of him at these moments is to fart loudly and he will run away from the awful smell.

Because there are so many spirits, some of them evil,

the Okinawans have many ways of protecting themselves from bad influences. One belief is that one powerful evil spirit can only travel in a straight line. Sometimes when this spirit hits a crossroads that dead-ends in front of a house, they believe it could enter the house and do harm to the people living there. So many crossroads have stone posts with three powerful *kanji* characters, 石敢當 (Ishiganto) written on them to protect them from evil. (Gaijinpot Blog)

Once again, I found myself encountering a worldview and set of beliefs and experiences that would have seemed very alien to the western culture in which I had grown up. I found them fascinating. Following are the stories of Tachan and Keiko as they told them to me.

Tachan

When Keiko and Tachan learned of my interest in ghost stories and hauntings, they explained to me that they both had the ability to sense and see spirits: Tachan, was, in fact a kind of shaman who was well versed in the supernatural history and lore of the islands where he had grown up.

Tachan (Tachan is his nickname. His real name is Tatsuya Shimojyo) told me that, from birth, he saw things *"differently, not in the usual way."* Then, when he was in his 20's, he had an accident. During surgery, while he was being examined for heart disease, the young woman doctor who was in charge made a mistake. According to Tachan, she *"wanted more experience"*, so she unnecessarily stuck a catheter into his heart in a kind of *"experiment"*. Tachan's heart stopped for 19 minutes and he came very near to dying. After he recovered, he found that he had acquired *"very strong shaman power"*.

Tachan had acquired the ability to sense and interact with the spiritual world. He could feel the presence of entities that were unseen by most people, and he became very aware of the forces, both beneficial and harmful, that emanated from various "power spots" on the islands where he lived. The hotel where we were staying on Sesoku Island was at the top of tall hill overlooking the ocean and the beached below. It was surrounded on all sides by traditional Okinawan tombs, which are huge circular stone or concrete structures shaped like a giant letter C. It is believed that the deity of the island is a Goddess, and these tombs represent her womb, and, symbolically, the womb of the island as well. When someone is born, they are believed to come from the Goddesses womb. When they die, they return to that same womb.

Tachan decided to show me the most powerful spot in the area. As we drove through the many tombs that surrounded our hotel, he pointed out one location off to the side of the road, which was dark looking and covered in stunted gnarled trees.

"Don't go there," he said. *"It's a very bad spot."* He raised his arm to point out the place, and I could see huge goose bumps rising on his skin.

"Very bad place," he repeated. He shivered as if he had been soaked in freezing water, and drove on.

As we drove, Tachan explained that there were many power spots in the area. The ones on Sesoku Island, where we were staying were mostly harmful and dangerous, whereas most of those on Motobu Island where we were going were good and benevolent.

We crossed the bridge separating the two islands, and, after a bit of searching on narrow country roads, he took me to Utaki, the strongest place of power in the area. After a few minutes of searching on small country roads, Tachan parked his van at the edge of some trees and led me down a small slope lined with large stones that served as an uneven stairway to the beach below.

After emerging from the trees, we found ourselves at the bottom of a slot canyon, a narrow stretch of pure white sand about 20 feet across flanked by steep cliffs of jagged black volcanic rock that rose to a height of about 60 feet on each side. The dark cliff sides were covered with jungle vines and flowers that nodded in the gentle sea breeze. The long corridor of white sand lead to the edge of the ocean, where lazy waves were lapping at the shoreline. The sand was bare, except in the middle of the long canyon where there stood one solitary black rock, about shoulder height, about six feet by four feet in length and breadth.

"The local people believe this rock is a Goddess who has power over this area," Tachan said, pointing at the solitary black stone standing in the pure white sand. *"It is a very good Goddess. This is the strongest power spot in the island, and you can get strength and good power from this place."*

On top of the stones, two huge seashells had been placed. Inside the seashells was a collection of small coins that visitors had placed there as offerings to the Goddess to grant their prayers. I placed a 100-yen coin inside the shell nearest me, and offered up my request for all the strength and good energy I could get.

The whole scene was a very dramatic statement of nature. The steep black cliffs full of razor sharp obsidian edges, contrasted sharply with the soft sand that seemed like spread sugar at our feet. The nodding palm trees at one end of the canyon, and the gentle lapping of the sea waves at the other gave a transcendent feeling of being in a sacred cathedral, treading a shining path before a squat black altar, with the dome of the blue sky above. Resting in the gentle sun, with the ocean breeze caressing your face, you felt refreshed and invigorated with the warm energy of the mysterious natural beauty that surrounded you. You had no doubt you were in the midst of a very sacred place.

Tachan explained that, at high tide, this entire canyon and the Goddess stone were completely under water, but, every day, it all emerged again from the salt water, washed clean and ready to bestow its blessings as it has for thousands of years.

We walked to the waters edge and stared silently out at the sea for a few moments. I looked to the right, gasped, and raised my camera. A surprised expression came across Tachan's face as he turned his head to follow my gaze.

"*Look, I said. "There, on the side of the cliff. It's a*

woman's face. *Do you see it?*" Tachan squinted his eyes, closely inspecting the cliff face and then gave a gasp of surprise. The entire cliff face on the right side of the canyon formed a rock formation that looked like the giant head of a woman gazing out to sea. From the expression on Tachan's face, I don't think he had ever noticed it before.

"*Yes, I see it,*" he said. I took several photographs before we left, feeling fully recharged and spiritually cleansed. The feeling lasted for several days after.

Tachan told me he could feel some kind of power coming from me. He said that I have a tendency to attract spiritual beings like ghosts, but that I tend to attract good things that give me strength and protect me. During the time when I was busy teaching at the hotel, Tachan told me he saw the spirit of a woman. He saw her three times. She walked out of the storage room next to the kitchen and over to where we were. He said she had long black hair and was wearing white clothing. He said she looked sad. He could feel that she wasn't dangerous or harmful: she was just there.

For a few days in a row, while I was resting in my room, I heard a sudden loud rap on the front of the clothes closet door. Twice it happened right next to where I was standing. I would look and see nothing there. Once when I was resting on my bed, I felt a hand grab my foot and gently tug on it as it trying to get my attention. But there was no one there I could see.

"*Don't worry,*" said Tachan. "*It's a good spirit. It likes you, and it will give you power.*"

Tachan did give me one warning, however. He said he was worried about me during this trip to Okinawa. He said that during my stay there, I should not enter any dense bush or forest, and to be careful what I touched while swimming in the sea. He said I was too curious and I might touch the wrong thing. He said something with strong poison, like a snake or something else would bite me and poison me both physically and spiritually. Okinawa is home to a number of dangerous creatures, including the deadly Habu snake, the venomous sea snake, the blue-ringed octopus, the lionfish and box jellyfish, each carrying its own type of wicked poison. I promised him I would be careful and promptly forgot about it as I enjoyed the times spent at the beach during breaks from teaching.

A couple days later, a group of students, teaching assistants and I were hanging out at one of the beaches of Sesoku Island. I was by myself, relaxing in the water at the edge of the beach, lying half submerged in the water under the blazing Okinawan sun. I lazily reached out my hand and dragged it through the water. My fingers struck something hard. I brushed away the sand around the object, closed my fingers around it, and brought it up where I could look at it.

I was holding a beautiful seashell about the size of my hand. It had various colors, brown, pink, magenta, running in thin bands around its width. As I stared at its fascinating shape and colors, I felt something push against my hand. I looked down to see a creature with long dark eyestalks emerging from the shell. The stalk eyes were looking directly at me as it flowed toward my hand.

I gasped and dropped the shell before it could touch me again. I didn't know why, but the encounter left me shaking and feeling very anxious. Later after returning to the hotel, I opened my laptop computer and began researching seashell creatures in Okinawa. I came across one with the same colors I had seen. It was the cone snail, which has one of the deadliest poisons known in nature. It is very capable of killing a human being, and there is no known antidote. I don't know for certain if what I was holding was, indeed, the venomous cone snail, but I am still very glad I dropped it and left it to go its own way in the gentle surf swelling along the beach on Sesoku Island.

Keiko

Keiko Hasegawa is the manager of the school that I taught for during the 12-day English seminar in Okinawa. She and Tachan are partners. When she learned of my interest in ghost stories, she surprised me by informing me that the school had previously rented a very large building on the neighboring island, where it had held its classes. Unfortunately, they had had to leave the building because it was so badly haunted that no one could stay there.

Like Tachan, Keiko's experience with the supernatural began at an early age. When she was a high school student, staying up late at night to study for her college entrance exam, one night she saw a dark shape standing at the bottom of the stairs that led to the second floor where she and her parents had their bedrooms. When she looked closer at the shape, she saw the shadow of a man in a long black coat with a hat on its head. She went back into her bedroom and tried to ignore it. But the next night, she saw it again, only closer, further up the stairs than before. For the next few nights after that, every time she opened her bedroom door at night, she saw the shadow man, closer each time she looked. She tried to tell her parents about it, but they wouldn't listen to her. When she kept insisting, they said she was crazy, probably under stress from too much studying. So she knew she would have to deal with it herself.

Finally, one night, she saw it was just outside her bedroom door, in front of her mother's room, which was next to hers. After she had shut her door to keep it out, she talked to it, shouting through her closed door, saying, "*You might live here, but don't come into my room! You are not welcome here. If you come in here, I will give you a punch!*"

The next night, her mother woke up from her sleep to find she couldn't move. She was experiencing a very strong *kinashibari*. She opened her eyes to see the shadow man bending over her with his hands on her throat. She struggled in terror until she could finally move again, and the shadow disappeared. She then immediately went to Keiko and apologized. "*I am sorry I didn't believe you,*" she said. "*The ghost was real!*"

The Hauntings at the Ie Jima School

Keiko had a plan to start her school on the Okinawan island of Ie Jima. It was very difficult at first for her to find a building for her business because she was from

Nagoya. When she first came there, she didn't know the island at all. The day she arrived, she asked the staff at the local business office if they knew of a building that she could rent for her business. They sent her to the Community Center and she was helped by one of the staff members, a lady who was very kind. She drove Keiko all around Ie Jima, but they couldn't find a good place on the island. Keiko was disappointed, and decided to go back to Nagoya. As the lady drove her to the airport, the lady suddenly said she had an idea about a place that might be good for her school. It was the Nowa Dojo, a former place for group meetings and seminars, which was not in use now.

Two days later, Keiko visited the offices of the Japan Agriculture Association, which owned the building. She asked the head of the Association about the building, and he took her there. It was a very old building, and very big. Keiko got a kind of creepy feeling while she was there, but she didn't pay any attention to it. For some reason, at first, many local dignitaries tried to block her getting the building. It took six months before she was allowed to rent it.

While everything was being arranged, she stayed one night in a guesthouse. One night, she met a construction worker who was also staying there. He asked her why she was there, and she told him about the building she was renting. He immediately called over several other construction workers who were staying there, and they told her the building was dangerous. They explained that everyone knew it was haunted, and she should be careful.

The next morning, Keiko was on her way to the port to

catch the ferry to the next island. She was a little late, so she was running. It was a very hot day, and she was sweating. Suddenly, a young girl appeared to her right. The girl looked to be about 11 years old. She had a bowl-shaped haircut and bangs, a very old style that is seldom seen these days. Keiko got a very cold feeling. She got goose bumps from her head down to her toes. The girl began to chase after her. Somehow Keiko knew she was a spirit from the haunted building she was renting.

Keiko stopped and talked to her. "*Don't follow me,*" she said. "*I can't do anything for you. I'm not from here.*" The girl turned and went back the other direction.

Keiko was worried about the building, but she decided she didn't care. She needed the place for her business. She decided to make peace with the ghosts there. She went to the building and spoke out loud to what ever was listening. She offered to make a contract.

"*If I can make a business here,*" she said, "*I will do my best to make this a prosperous place. It is so gloomy here now.*"

Then she spoke directly to the girl she had seen on the road. "*If you allow me to rent and use this building, I will plant some beautiful yellow hydrangeas in the garden for you and the others who are here.*"

But she forgot to plant them. She and Tachan, her partner, started doing renovations to the building. It took along time, and even after eight months, they were not finished. Then many strange problems began to happen. She hired a carpenter from Nagoya and brought him there. He was very experienced at his job, but very old, and after a while, he began to look ill: his face looked like a skeleton. Then at one part of the building that he had already finished, an entire wall suddenly fell down. As a result, she couldn't use that room for seminars during the first semester of her school. She fired the carpenter, and he returned to Nagoya.

She and Tachan continued the renovations on their own. One day Keiko was standing on the top of a tall ladder, caulking the ceiling, when she missed a rung and fell. She landed on her side and broke three bones in her legs into six pieces. As she was falling through the air, she heard a man's voice in her ear that said, "*Don't ride the horses!*" She was shocked because she was about to begin horseback riding at a local club. She had already bought the entire outfit and boots – everything except the helmet. She decided later not to try this new hobby.

She returned to Nagoya to recover. Afterwards, when she returned to Ie Jima, she planted the yellow hydrangeas and continued with her work at the school.

Keiko soon noticed that everybody who was staying or spending time in the building began to change. At first she had a business partner, a man from Canada. He changed from being very positive and active to being difficult and contentions. He soon left because of personal troubles. She felt herself changing as well. She felt depressed and anxious. She began to lose weight. She had weighed 50 kilograms when she moved there, but she soon was down to 43. Her friends back in Nagoya were worried about her when they saw her photos. Tachan told her the spirits were stealing her energy.

Tachan felt very strongly that there was something very wrong about the place. He told her, "*If you stay here, the bad spirit will pull out your eyes*". This was in reference to a local saying that states, "*If you are trapped by a bad spirit, then your eyes cannot see*". A short time later, Keiko inexplicably lost the vision in her right eye. Luckily it was only temporary and her vision soon returned.

Keiko hired a teacher to help with the classes. One day the teacher came to her and said, "*Please don't laugh at me, but I want to tell you something*". She said twice she had seen the ghost of a man standing in the hallway. She said it wasn't a Japanese man. They both figured he might be the ghost of an American who had been killed there during World War II. When the Americans invaded Okinawa, Ie Jima was the first island they landed on. There had been bitter fighting all around the area where her school now stood.

A short while later, one evening Keiko was in her room preparing for the next day's class. She looked up to see a man walk across her room, emerging from one wall, and then disappearing into another.

Keiko hired a teacher from the Philippines. She had been hired to teach for one month, and she arrived with her children, looking forward to their stay in Okinawa. During conversation together, Keiko learned that this lady was well known as a kind of shaman who was believed to have strong spiritual power back in her home area. But she went back home after only two days, before she had even started teaching.

She claimed a large number of ghosts had appeared to her and warned, "*Don't take anything from this building.*"

She said she argued with the spirits, "*I have a right to take my salary. If I don't, how can I take care of my children?*" She had been divorced and was raising them alone. She said the ghosts would not relent. So she left without even taking any salary.

She told Keiko she had seen many gray figures standing together in the garden. She said they looked very strong. They wanted to rush forward and come into the school. In the middle of all of these gray figures, she said she saw the figure of a lady dressed in white who was trying to calm the gray ones and hold them back. The Filipina said the number of gray figures was growing every day. She didn't know how much longer the white lady could hold them back. She told Keiko to take care of the yellow hydrangea flowers in the garden, as they had a good and calming effect on the spirits there.

Keiko had a cat that she had brought from Nagoya. It had been her companion for many years. She said the cat began to act strange. Even the look in its eyes changed. She said it would no longer come to her, but just sat in the corner looking at her. It refused to stay with her in her bedroom at night.

Keiko began to hear strange sounds. She often heard the sound of big boots walking back and forth outside her window at midnight. When she looked out the window, there was no one there. Sometimes in the daytime, in whatever room she was in, the windows and doors would begin to vibrate and rattle loudly for no reason she could see.

One day a local *noro* showed up at her school. There are 2 types of spiritual guides that are common in Okinawa, both of which are usually female: the *yuta* and the *noro*. A *yuta* is similar to what the rest of Japan calls a *reibaishi*, and in the west we call a spiritual medium or a channeler. The *yuta* talks with the spirits of the dead and listens to what they have to say. The *noro* is something different. A *noro* is a type of priestess who talks directly to the Gods. They have there own Goddess that they pray to, which is female. The island of Ie Jima also has its own female deity, and the *noros* there pray to their Goddess, who then intercedes for them with the major Goddess of the island.

Keiko had heard that there was a powerful *noro* in the area, but she had never met her. The *noro* turned up unannounced and said, "I heard you are in trouble, and I have come to help you". It turned out that this *noro* was a relative of one of Keiko's friends. The friend had told her relative about the strange happenings at the school.

The *noro* was 87 years old. After a time, she and Keiko became close friends. The *noro* explained to Keiko some reasons why she was having so much trouble. She told her everyone in the area knew that the building she was in was a bad power spot. The island of Ie Jima was a power spot itself, and the small mountain that the school sat on amplified the power. The place where the school stood was full of bad energy, all of which made the spiritual power there almost overwhelming. The *noro* admitted that even she was afraid to go there, but she wanted to help Keiko, so she would try.

The *noro* tried 3 times to quiet the spirits that were bothering Keiko at the school. The first time, she had to visit 4 holy spots on the island to prepare herself for the encounter with the spirits there.

When she came to the school, she walked around the building many times chanting holy words. Her purpose was to calm the spirits there so Keiko could live there in peace. he walked around the building chanting until she thought she had succeeded. For a while after that, things were quiet at the school, but soon Keiko began to hear the same sounds that had frightened her before.

The *noro* came a second time, with the same result. At first, quiet, and then the disturbances began again stronger than before.

Before she came the third time, the *noro* told Keiko that she was afraid to try again. She felt she wasn't strong enough to fight what was there, and she was pretty sure she would be hurt if she came there again, but she wanted very much to help her friend. So she came one more time and did her best to quiet the spirits. After she went home, she fell down and broke her leg.

Soon Keiko began to experience strange feelings at night, which prevented her from sleeping. She would be in her big bed with her dog or cat, and then she would feel the presence of many people surrounding her and looking at her. She always woke up at about 2:00 AM, and heard the voices of many people talking all around her.

She sometimes saw a shadow in the shape of a man moving down the hallway. Two of her friends who had come to visit told her that they had also seen the ghost of a man, sometimes looking in the window at them, or moving down the hallways.

The final breaking point came when she was walking down the hallway one day near the rooms they used as classrooms. There was no one else in the building, as that semester's classes had finished. She saw a bright orange light flashing in one of the rooms. The light seemed to be filling the whole room. She ran to the room and looked in, but nothing was there. After that, she decided to leave.

She was worried about how she would get out of the lease she had signed when she had first rented the building. She was legally liable for several more years of rent. But when she went to the Agriculture Association that owned the building, they acted as if they had been expecting to see her. They said they knew all about the strange things that went on in that building: nobody local would go near the place. They agreed to let her out of her lease, and she moved out as quickly as she could. The building still stands empty to this day.

As a kind of addendum to the story of the haunted school, I would like to share this message I received from Keiko a short while ago:

I heard today that the local people of Ie island cut down almost all the big trees at the ghost building. The JA Company is trying to invite some tourists to stay there as like a guest house. So I assume they thought if there aren't big trees and the garden seems like light with the sun, some tourists will be able to stay there. However I believe they shouldn't have cut off the trees. It must start some unusual things happening soon.

Ghost Footprints Outside My Door

I currently teach at a university in Nagoya, Japan. I have an office on the sixth floor, which is comfortable and useful for meeting students and colleagues. I use when doing research, class planning, and writing. I feel at home there with all of my books stacked on the shelves and my favorite photos on the wall. It has an atmosphere of being "my sacred space", which I appreciate very much. Seminar rooms and the offices of other professors take up the rest of the sixth floor. I was in residence at this university for two years with nothing unusual happening to me, although one teacher from Jamaica whose office was down the hall reported that she had been obliged to chase some kind of strange spirit out of her office room, the story of which is told the earlier, "Gaijn and Ghosts," chapter of this book ("Venicia's Story").

Sometime during my third year at the university, one of the professors from America knocked on my door and called me out into the hall. "*Have you seen this?*" he asked. He pointed to the floor and there, placed squarely on a floor tile in front of my office door, was a human footprint. It was someone's right bare foot, situated so that it looked like it had just walked out of the door of my office.

We looked at it with the astonishment it deserved. It had certainly not been there previously. Where had it come from? As we examined it more closely, we became even more baffled by this strange phenomenon. The first question that came to mind was, who had been walking barefoot from my office that I was unaware of? And why barefoot?

When we looked closer, the mystery only deepened. It was not just a print, but it was bulging UP out of the solid floor tile as if someone had stepped on the underside of it and made a deep impression pointing upward. The hallway flooring consisted of solid linoleum floor tiles placed on top of a metal floor. How was it possible for an impression of a bare foot to be pushing up out of a solid floor tile? The person who made it would have had to have been walking shoeless on the ceiling of the fifth floor leaving an impression that pushed up all the way through solid steel and linoleum. Try as we might, we could think of no logical explanation for what we were looking at.

I soon learned to just accept the footprint as part of my office landscape, and went about my business. Soon however, I bean to hear an occasional loud rap coming form the front of my office, as if someone were knocking with a fist hard upon the wall. Several times I got up and went to my door, but there was never anyone there. It was the same every time. One loud knock on the wall, and then silence. Soon I was hearing the rap almost every day, sometimes several times a day. I had experienced such things many times before, however, so I just accepted it and went on with my teaching.

About two years later, I was walking down the hallway to my office, when I happened to glance down at the floor, and was stopped in my tracks by what I saw. There, next to the ghostly footprint that had been sitting outside my office, was a second footprint that had appeared beside it. It was almost identical to the first one: someone's shoeless right foot, placed as it was striding out of my office door. My fellow teachers and I examined it as closely as we could. Once again, we could find no logical explanation as to how it had gotten there.

"This could only happen to you," the Jamaican lady said to me as she shook her head in wonder. Many of the other teachers knew about my many encounters with strange phenomena, and my interest in the supernatural. After a few weeks, a third footprint began to appear, but thus far it is only showing the front toes of the foot. Many of my friends found time to stop by and shake their heads at the footprints, but none could offer any explanation as what had made them, or where they had come from. The rapping on my front wall became a daily occurrence, and life went on.

In one final weird chapter to this story, I decided I would like a photo of the footprints as proof of what I was talking about when I told the story of the footprints to other people. I was unable to get a clear photo, however, as the lighting in the hallway is very bad, and a flash photograph simply blurred out the prints, making it difficult to see them.

I asked a friend who is a professional photographer to help me out. He came to my office, set up special lighting, used several different lenses and exposure settings, but was unable to get anything but a flat, barely discernable image. Finally, we gave up on the project, went out and had a drink, and had a great conversation about the supernatural and the many mysteries in the world.

Two weeks later, I was working late in my office. After I finished up, I grabbed my coat, shut off the lights in my room, and opened the door. I stopped and stared in wonder at the sight that greeted me just outside my office door. There, at my feet, all three (or should I say all two and a half?) footprints were glowing brightly in a soft golden light. The hallway outside my office is long and badly lighted with dim fluorescent lighting. At the far end of the hallway, about 30 feet away, is a very small window, about two feet tall and half a foot in width. In what was perhaps a very rare event, the glowing sundown taking place on the far horizon was hitting the window squarely, sending a long beam of golden light down the hallway that fell directly on the spot where the footprints lay, bathing them in a soft golden light that revealed every detail. Knowing that this situation would not last very long, I took out my cell phone and used its tiny camera to get the picture I had been trying so hard to take before. If you ask me, I will be glad to show it to you, or you can visit my office and see the footprints for yourself. If you can come up with a logical explanation of where they came from, or what is rapping on my office wall, I will be glad to hear it.

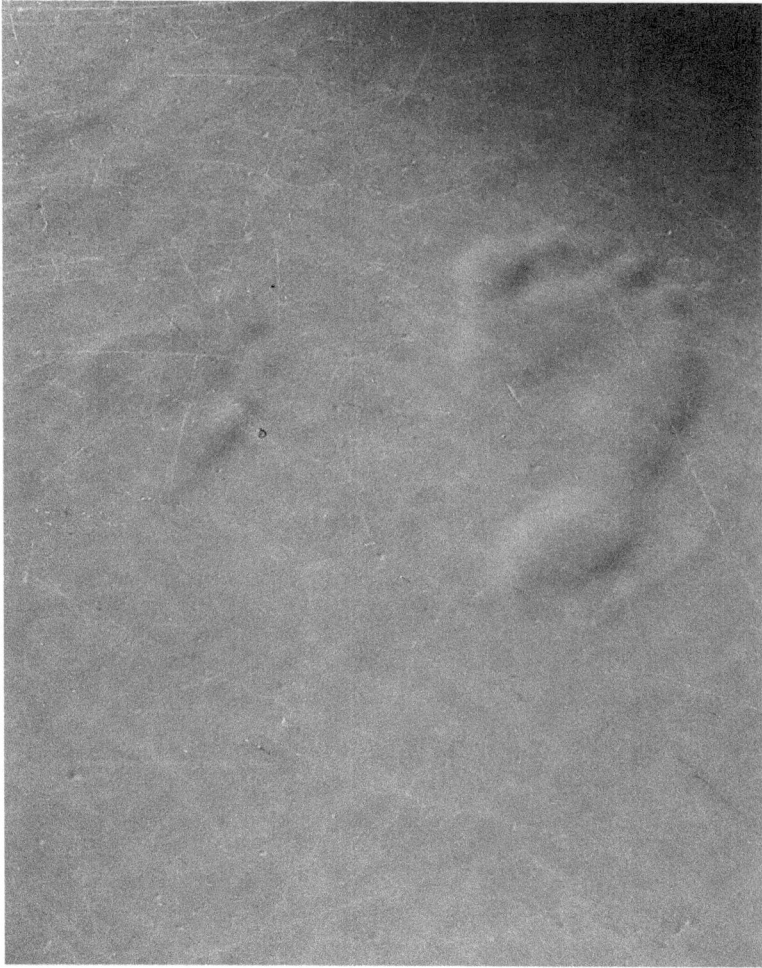

About Thomas Bauerle

Thomas Bauerle has lived in Japan and Asia for 30 years. He teaches Writing and American Culture at Nagoya City University.

He graduated from Indiana University, USA with an MFA in Creative Writing. He has published magazine articles and short stories in many publications, including: *Brilliant Corners*, *Avenues* and *Japanzine*, where he was a winner of the "Sudden Fiction" contest.

He has had many encounters with the strange and the paranormal in his life. One story he wrote about when he lived in a house that was haunted by a young woman who hanged herself in the 1930s was published in the book, *Forty Stories of Japan*. After he was presented with this book the Japanese ambassador to New Zealand commented, *"It was my favorite story in the book. It reminded me of old Japan."* Two of his true ghost stories were recently published in the International Writers magazine *Emanations*. The literary blogger Dario Rivarossa mentioned them in his blog "The Best Ghost Stories" as: *"Some very fine and true stories."*

He continues to pursue the mysterious and the spiritual aspects of the world in which we live.

A Glossary of Japanese Words:

bonenkai: An end of the year or "forget the old year" party. Usually involves drinking and eating with friends.

Bosatsu: A Buddhist saint who has reached the highest level of enlightenment, but chooses to remain here on the earthly plane to help other people.

Bunshinsaba: A form of divination popular with young Japanese and Koreans in which letters and numbers are written on a piece of paper, similar in style to an Ouija Board. Two people hold a pen over the paper and ask questions, and the pen moves in a form of spirit writing to spell out the answers. The pen is supposedly controlled by the ghost of "Bunshinsaba", a young girl who was murdered. The practice first became popular in Korea, and then became known to Japanese through the Korean horror movie "Bunshinsaba", in which Korean high school students call up the ghost using this method.

butsudan: A traditional Japanese altar honoring dead family ancestors, which is found in many Japanese homes. It usually consists of pictures of family members that have passed on. Candles are lit and food and drink is offered to the souls of the departed while prayers are offered up asking for their help and guidance.

butsudana: The room in which the *butsudan*, or traditional Japanese altar to the dead is kept.

danshi: Spare apartment usually supplied by a Japanese company for its workers to live in.

duppy: Jamaican word for a ghost.

Hatsumode: The first visit to a Shinto shrine or Buddhist temple at the beginning of the New Year. It is traditional for the Japanese to visit on or soon after New Years day to pray for good luck in the coming year.

hito-dana: A "spirit fireball" or "corpse-candle". A floating ball of fire that is thought to be the soul of someone newly dead.

hikui: A low, deep-sounding voice.

itai!: Ouch! That hurts!

ju-mon: An ancient charm or incantation in Sanskrit that originated in India in the early days of Buddhism. Used to protect from evil and exorcise ghosts.

kami-dana: A shrine to Shinto Gods in the home. It often consists of a tiny house for the Gods of the home to stay in, and receptacles in front where daily offerings of salt, sake, and a green plant are placed to keep the Gods happy.

kami-shimo: Traditional samurai clothing that included baggy pants.

Kannon, or Kannon-sama: The Buddhist Goddess of Mercy, often invoked by priests during exorcisms or to help and protect people who are being bothered by evil spirits or ghosts.

Kannon-giyo Sutra: An ancient sutra recited by a priest to invoke the power of Kannon, the Buddhist Goddess of Mercy to come and give protection from evil.

kanashibari: A ghost that comes to people in their sleep and holds them down so they can't move. Often, besides being held immobile, the victim of a kanashibari will also hear voices, and be approached by various spiritual entities.

kanji: The ancient Chinese pictographs adopted by the Japanese into their writing system. Sometimes the number of brush strokes used to write a person's fortunetellers to tell the customer's future use name in kanji.

Kijimuna: An impish ogre, who is believed to reside in the forests of Okinawa. *Kijimuna*, who is usually depicted with bright red hair and a purple face, is a trickster being who plays pranks on people if they offend him, or if he is not appeased in the proper way.

kimodameshi: To test a person's courage by daring them to do something dangerous or risky. Often young Japanese test each other to see who is the bravest by going at night to known haunted sites.

Kokkuri-san, or Kokkuri-sama: Kokkuri-san is the Japanese Fox God who is known for his mischievousness. Young Japanese often play a game similar to the *Ouija Board* known in the west, where they write the Japanese *hiragana* alphabet on a piece of paper, sometimes with *hai* (yes), *ie* (no), and the numbers 1 to 10. Then a five yes coin, which has a hole in the middle, is placed on the paper and two people put their fingertips on the coin. The spirit of *Kokkurisan* is called up and then asked questions. The coin, touched by the spirit of *Kokkurisan*, moves across the paper, spelling out the answers. It is a very popular game with Japanese Junior high and high school students.

menshuku: A small traditional Japanese inn.

makai-bi: The tradition of lighting a fire to guide the family ancestors' ghosts back to heaven at the end of Japanese *O-Bon* festival for the dead.

Noro: A type of shaman or holy person, usually female, unique to Okinawa. The *noro* has a special deity or Goddess that she talks to who advises her and gives her the power to perform exorcisms, and help people who need her assistance.

Yuta: A type of shaman, or holy person, usually female, unique to Okinawa. The *yuta* talks with and gets advice from the spirits of the dead in order to help and advise people who need her help. The *yuta* might be compared with the spiritual medium or channeler in western culture, or the *reibaishi* in other parts of Japan.

Works Cited

Gaijinpot Blog, "Weird Superstitions from Okinawa." file:///Users/thomasbauerle/Desktop/Weird%20and%20W onderful%20Superstitions%20from%20Okinawa.htm

Moore, Nolan. "Ten Scientific Explanations for Ghostly Phenomena." *Weird Stuff.* September 30, 2013. Retrieved from http://listverse.com/2013/09/30/10-scientific-explanations-for-ghostly-phenomena/

Sacks, Oliver. *Hallucinations.* New York: Alfred A. Knopf, 2012. Print

Taylor, Troy. *The Ghost Hunter's Handbook.* Chicago: Whitechapel Press. 2010. Print

"The Science of Ghosts and Hauntings." *The Museum of Unnatural History.* Retrieved from http://www.unmuseum.org/ghosts.htm

Wicks, Cheryl A., with Ed and Lorraine Warren. *Ghost Tracks.* Bloomington, Indiana: Authorhouse. 2004. Print

Notes:

The section "Keeping the Sprit's Happy; An Interview With a Buddhist Faith Healer" originally appeared in

Bauerle, Thomas. "Keeping the Spirits Happy: An

Interview With a Buddhist faith Healer." *Avenues*, Nagoya, Japan. January: 1995. Pages 10-12. Print

The sections, "Norie's Story" and "Michiyo's Story" first appeared in:

Bauerle, Thomas. "True Japanese Ghost Stories." *Emanations*, Carter Kaplan, ed. Brookline, Massachusetts: International Authors. 2014. Pages 359-366. Print

The sections, "Mark's Apartment," "Noel and the Exorcist," Yoko's Story," Ghost Hotel," and "Kokkuri-san: Ghost Hotel," all first appeared in:

Bauerle, Thomas. "True Tales of Haunts, Horrors and Exorcists." *Avenues*, Nagoya, Japan: September, 1993. Pages 6-9. Print

A slightly different version of the section, "My Life With the Ghost Lady" first appeared in:

Bauerle, Thomas. "Living With the Ghost Lady", essay published in *Forty Stories of Japan*. Fine Line Press, New Zealand 2010. Print.

Other Books From Asteroth's Books

Asteroth's Books publishes books about ghosts, the paranormal, and other strange topics.... Here is a selection of other titles available.

G. Michael Vasey
The Black Eyed Demons Are Coming (*Kindle*)
Ghosts of the Living (*Kindle*)
True Tales of Haunted Places (*Kindle*)
The Most Haunted Country in the World – The Czech Republic (*Kindle and paperback*)
The Black-Eyed Kids (*Kindle and audio*)
Your Haunted Lives – Revisited (*Kindle and Audio book*)
Ghosts In The Machines (*Kindle and audio book*)
How To Create Your Own Reality (*Paperback and Kindle*)
God's Pretenders – Incredible Tales of Magic and Alchemy (*Kindle and audio book*)
My Haunted Life – Extreme Edition (*Paperback, audiobook and Kindle*)
The Mystical Hexagram (*Paperback and Kindle*)

Sam White
Will We Meet Again? (*Kindle*)

http://www.asterothsbooks.com

* 9 7 8 0 9 9 6 1 9 7 2 5 0 *